Journey Through the Psalms
A Path to Wholeness

Kaleidoscope

Statement of Purpose

Kaleidoscope is a series of adult educational resources developed for the ecumenical church by Lancaster Theological Seminary and the United Church Board for Homeland Ministries. Developed for adults who want serious study and dialogue on contemporary issues of Christian faith and life, Kaleidoscope offers elective resources designed to provide new knowledge and new understanding for persons who seek personal growth and a deeper sense of social responsibility in their lives.

Kaleidoscope utilizes the expertise of professionals in various disciplines to develop study resources in both print and video. The series also provides tools to help persons develop skills in studying, reflecting, inquiring critically, and exploring avenues of appropriate Christian responses in life.

Kaleidoscope provides sound and tested resources in theology, biblical studies, ethics, and other related subjects that link personal growth and social responsibility to life situations in which adult Christian persons develop.

Journey Through the Psalms

A Path to Wholeness

Denise Dombkowski Hopkins

A Kaleidoscope Series Resource

United Church Press
New York

To

My brother, Brian S. Dombkowski
June 7, 1955 to September 3, 1978

I miss you.

KALEIDOSCOPE SERIES

Scripture quotations where noted are from the Revised Standard Version of the Bible, copyrighted 1946, 1952, © 1971, 1973, by the Division of Christian Education of the National Council of Churches of Christ in the United States of America, and are used by permission. All other quotations are translations by the author. Permission is given in the Leader's Guide edition to reproduce only the author's discussion questions for group use.

Additional acknowledgment of permissions is found in the Notes section of this volume.

Library of Congress Cataloging-in-Publication Data

Hopkins, Denise Dombkowski.
    Journey through the Psalms : a path to wholeness / Denise Dombkowski Hopkins.
        p.   cm.   —(A Kaleidoscope series resource)
Includes bibliographical references.
    ISBN 0-8298-0875-2 : $5.95.   —   ISBN 0-8298-0876-0 (leader's guide)
: $6.95
    1. Bible. O.T. Psalms—Study.   I. Title.   II. Series.
BS1451.H66 1990
223' .2'00712—dc20   90-46946
                                                                          CIP

This book is printed on acid-free, recycled paper to save trees and help preserve the earth.

United Church Press, 475 Riverside Drive, New York, N.Y. 10115

Contents

How to Use the Kaleidoscope Series

The Kaleidoscope book is the basic resource for all students in the Kaleidoscope Series. For each Kaleidoscope book there is a Leader's Guide edition, which has a sixteen-page Leader's Guide bound into the back of the book. The leader will need to study both the text and the Leader's Guide to prepare to lead study sessions of the Kaleidoscope Series resources. The video is a very helpful tool for the leader and the class when using this book as a study resource.

Other KALEIDOSCOPE Resources are:

- **BREAD FOR THE BANQUET: Experiencing Life in the Spirit,** by Elaine M. Ward
- **THE GIFT AND THE PROMISE: Becoming What We Are in Christ,** by Peter Schmiechen
- **GOD, WHERE ARE YOU? Suffering and Faith,** by Richard F. Vieth
- **NOBODY'S CHILD: A Generation Caught in the Middle,** by Paul E. Irion
- **STRETCH OUT YOUR HAND: Exploring Healing Prayer,** by Tilda Norberg and Robert D. Webber
- **THUNDER ON THE RIGHT: Understanding Conservative Christianity,** by Elizabeth C. Nordbeck

Introduction to the Kaleidoscope Series

Through direct experience, our faculty at Lancaster Theological Seminary discovered that a continual demand exists for Christian theological reflection upon issues of current interest. To meet this demand, the Seminary for many years has offered courses for lay people. To offer the substance of these courses to the wider Christian public is the purpose of the Kaleidoscope Series.

Lancaster Seminary exists to proclaim the gospel of Jesus Christ for the sake of the church and the world. In addition to preparing men and women for the ordained Christian ministry, the Seminary seeks to be a center of theological reflection for clergy and laity. Continuing education and leadership development for all Christians focus our mission. The topics and educational style in the Kaleidoscope Series extend Lancaster Seminary's commitment: theological study reflective of the interaction of the Bible, the world, the church, worship, and personal faith. We hope that this course will provide an opportunity for you to grow in self-understanding, in knowledge of other people and God's creation, and in the spirit of Christ.

We wish to thank the staff of the Division of Education and Publication of the United Church Board for Homeland Ministries for their support in this enterprise. The Rev. Dr. Ansley Coe Throckmorton, The Rev. Dr. Larry E. Kalp, and The Rev. Dr. Percel O. Alston provided encouragement and support for the project. In particular, we are grateful for the inspiration of Percel Alston, who was a trustee of Lancaster Seminary. His life-long interest in adult education makes it most appropriate that this series be dedicated to him. Two other staff members have guided the series through the writing and production stages: The Rev. Willard Wetzel, Project Coordinator for the Kaleidoscope Series, and The Rev. Nancy G. Wright, Editor for Kaleidoscope. As a publishing staff they have provided valuable experience and counsel. Finally, I wish to recognize the creative leadership of Mrs. Jean Vieth, the Seminary Coordinator for the Series, who has been active for several years in this educational program at Lancaster.

Peter M. Schmiechen, President
The Lancaster Theological Seminary

Chapter 1

Who Needs the Psalms Anyway? We've Got Our Hymnals!

The Psalms as a Part of Our Christian Heritage

Why should we study the psalms of ancient Israel? Do Christians today need the Book of Psalms when, after all, it is our hymnals that provide prayer and song for worship? Although the hymnbook is a relatively modern development, it seems to have displaced rather than supplemented the psalms in today's worship. We may encounter some psalms cut and pasted in the back of our hymnals as responsive readings; religious houses may pray psalms faithfully daily; and liturgical reforms among some denominations may have recovered the use of psalms in eucharistic liturgies. But by and large, for too many Christians the psalms are not preached from, prayed from, or sung in worship services nor studied in Bible studies as much as they could be. Psalms are often treated as no more than poetic appendages to our liturgies or as catchy introductions to church committee meetings. For most of us, psalms—and only certain favorites at that!—function at best as the vehicle of our private devotions and meditations.

The psalms deserve our attention and renewed use in worship for several reasons. First, as much as our hymnals have shaped our

Christian identity, it is the Book of Psalms, not the hymnbook, that has been part of the worship of the church from the very beginning. The Psalter was the hymnbook of Second Temple Judaism and of the early church, which read the psalms as scripture, recited them as prayers, and sang them as hymns. Psalms were taken up by the later church for use in liturgies and the Daily Offices. Saints, mystics, and monks through the centuries have turned to the psalms as their devotional book. The hymnody of the reformers drew heavily from the psalms.

In order to understand who we are as worshiping Christians, we must reclaim our psalm heritage. To do that is to stand today in continuity with our tradition, in touch with our roots. In this sense then "the Psalms are something like a family album; they remind us of who we are and of things that happened to us."[1] They tell and reflect our own story.

Second, because the psalms are the common heritage of all churches, they provide a ready base for ecumenical worship. It is no accident, for example, that psalms permeated the worship book of the Sixth Assembly of the World Council of Churches.[2] The psalms can also provide nourishment for the spiritual hunger that so many Christians across the ecumenical spectrum are experiencing. As a trip to any bookstore will substantiate, new translations and paraphrases of, meditations on, and musical settings for the psalms appear with regularity. This interest testifies to the yearning for renewal of worship and prayer in our time. That many of these works have little or nothing in common with the Hebrew text of the psalms, however, ought to warn us against too readily digesting such spiritual junk food. The psalms cannot say whatever we want them to say, but a careful study of the psalms can contribute to a faithful renewal of the worship life of contemporary Christians.

For many Christians, unfortunately, there remains nothing but a "spiritual vacuum"[3] at the center of their lives, into which has rushed a flood of prayer pamphlets and "a religious form of do-it-yourself techniques for helping people cope."[4] This situation is caused, in part, by the split within much of contemporary theology between the doctrine of God (theology) and prayer. A third reason, then, to reappropriate the psalms is to reunite theology and prayer. Psalm prayer can serve as a criterion for the "prayability" of our doctrine of God: "Is this a God to whom we can pray in the full range of biblical prayer?"[5]

Rather than move from a systematic and theoretical construct of God to prayer and our experience, the community of faith needs to move also in the opposite direction. Does the experience of different people, as it is articulated in prayer, square with the picture of God that theology has sketched? If not, then what becomes of that experience? Must it be denied or negated? Can a person be whole before God in the face of such denial? Can one group of people control another group of people with a picture of God (a theology) that denies the experience of the other group? Prayer and theology go together; loss of their dialectical relationship can lead to the atrophy of both and an erosion of the community of faith.

Perhaps most important, the psalms warrant our renewed interest because they offer us what Roland Murphy calls "a school of prayer," not simply in the sense of a collection of prayers, but rather as lessons in how to pray.[6] The psalms teach us that there are many different kinds of prayer and many different ways of praying to God that articulate the whole range of human emotions: fear, praise, anger, thanksgiving, joy, despair. All of the emotions that mark a person's struggle for faith from day to day appear in the Psalter. Psalm language grasps for us the many facets of God and our relationship to God, whom we experience as both present and absent.

Unfortunately, the church has been quite selective in designing our curriculum in this "school of prayer" that is the psalms. Despite the fact that more than one third of the Psalter contains lament psalms, Christian tradition has drawn heavily only from the seven penitential laments (Psalms 6, 32, 38, 51, 102, 130, and 143), especially during the lenten season. Though not denying the need for penitential lament, Murphy wonders "if we have lost the art of complaining *in faith* to God in favor of a stoic concept of what obedience or resignation to the divine will really means."[7]

Without the angry laments, we are cut off from the opportunity to be honest and whole in our prayer before God. As Walter Brueggemann insists, "The one-sided liturgical renewal of today, has, in effect, driven the hurtful side of experience either into obscure corners of faith practice or completely out of Christian worship"; the church's "failure of nerve" regarding the lament is clear.[8] Gordon Lathrop argues similarly that "it is a biblical, liturgical goal to let lament into the center of our assemblies. Nothing else is appropriate for the 20th century."[9]

The psalm lament certainly extends what the church has too often seen to be the traditional range of prayer. That the church has restricted our praying of the psalms in worship is clear from a glance at the responsive psalm readings in the back of most hymnals. I call this the scissors-and-paste method of liturgical psalm use. When angry laments *are* used, the guts of the lament are cut out, and we go immediately from petition to praise, skipping over the angry questions.[10]

Not only is our prayer challenged by the psalms, but so is our hymn singing. Though many of the songs in our hymnals claim to be based upon particular psalms, a comparison between hymn and psalm often shows that the two have little in common except for a few words or phrases. What is at issue here is not the christological interpretation of the psalms but rather a basic misinterpretation of the theology (talk about God) and the anthropology (talk about human beings) of the psalms.

Preaching in our churches has also suffered from the clergy's unwillingness to embrace the entire psalm range as the stuff of proclamation.[11] Erhard Gerstenberger, for example, boldly challenges Christian preachers to take up the theme of enemies and evildoers in the laments as "one of the most crucial issues of our times." The "enemy" problem has not disappeared today but has simply been reformulated in our mechanistic, impersonal world. We must ask today who is responsible for suffering and dehumanization. Christians have kept few church services to help the individual and the community in suffering or in naming and dealing with "enemies." Only to the extent in which worship "includes or embraces present-day reality" can our Sunday services claim to "represent the heart of a Christian congregation."[12] In light of Gerstenberger's challenge, we must ask, When was the last time a pastor preached from a psalm in worship? Is "enemies" language simply rejected as "unchristian"?

If we cannot pray the full range of psalm prayer, if our hymns distort the meaning of the psalms, if we do not hear psalms proclaimed from the pulpit, then the psalms are not functioning as fully for us as they ought. We are being cut off from a valuable resource for our liturgy, devotional life, and pastoral care of one another. A journey through the psalms can be a path to whole-ness, healing, and rootedness. The psalms engage our whole person. They demand our aesthetic response to the beauty of the poetry, our theological response to the picture of God that is drawn, and our emotional response to the humanness of the psalmists. Psalms speak "both *for* us as they express our thoughts and feelings, fears and hopes, and *to* us as we hear in them direction for the life of faith and something of God's way with us."[13] To sing the psalms, pray them, and hear them preached calls us to continuity with our tradition and joins us with other Christians past and present in the struggle for faith in God.

A Brief History of Psalm Use in the Church

In the New Testament there are at least 100 quotations from more than sixty of the psalms. Among the sayings of Jesus in the Gospels, there are more quotations from Psalms than from any other book of Hebrew Scripture (Deuteronomy and Isaiah follow in number of quotations). For example, Jesus uses Psalms 22 (Mark 15:34), 31 (Luke 23:46), and 69 at Calvary, quotes 110, 118, and 41 in his teaching, and sings the Hallel Psalms (113–118) in the upper room (Mark 14:26). The evangelists used many psalm texts in reference to Jesus' baptism and temptation, his ministry and teaching, and especially his passion. Peter in Acts 2:25–35, in his sermon at the church's first Pentecost, cited texts from Joel and Psalms 16, 132, and 110 as pointing to Christ's resurrection and ascension. Paul christologizes the Psalter in his thirty-one refer-ences to it, orienting it to the event of Jesus Christ and faith in him as Messiah.[14] Revelation alludes to the Psalter, especially to Psalms 113 through 118.

This frequent use of the Hebrew Scripture psalms in the New Testament does not mean that the early Christian church com-posed no psalms or hymns of its own. Many sayings of Jesus in the Gospels are in poetic form, notably the Beatitudes, and many of the discourses in John. There are many hymn fragments scattered throughout the New Testament, for example, the Magnificat in Luke 1:46–55, the Benedictus (Canticle of Zechariah) in Luke 1:68–79, and the Philippian hymn in Philippians 2:6–11. These have found a permanent place in the liturgies of the church. It is not likely, however, that these Christian hymns displaced the psalms, which were reinterpreted by the church in the light of the Christ event.

Where did these early Christians get their knowledge of the psalms? From the Hebrew Scriptures, which were their "Bible," and from the public worship in the Temple and the synagogue, where Jews met for worship and instruction on the sabbath and during the week. The Books of 1 and 2 Chronicles ostensibly record the organization of choirs in the time of David and Solomon (1 Chronicles 6:31–48), but more probably they give us information about the Second Temple (built after the return from Babylonian exile, 520–515 B.C.E., and destroyed by the Romans in 70 C.E.) and its worship. The names of some choir guilds are found in several psalm superscriptions (that is, titles written above the psalms): Asaph (50, 73–83); the children of Korah (42–49, 84–85, 87–88); Heman (88; see 1 Chronicles 25:6, which suggests that the sons *and daughters* of Heman were "all under the direction of their father . . . in the house of the Lord"); Ethan (89); and Jeduthun (39, 62, 77). In the Second Temple, psalms were sung by choirs of priest singers from the tribe of Levi (Levites), whose job was to supervise temple worship; they were to "play loudly on musical instruments, on harps and lyres and cymbals, to raise sounds of joy [1 Chron. 15:16]"; (compare with 2 Chronicles 5:13; 7:6). At various places in the singing and playing of instruments, people responded with praise shouts of hallelujah or refrains, for example, "For God's ḥesed endures forever [2 Chron. 5:13]."[15]

The superscriptions, or titles written above a few psalms, indicate their liturgical use in the Temple. The superscription of Psalm 100, for example, reads *mizmor letodah,* a song accompanied by a stringed instrument for the *todah,* or thanksgiving sacrifice; see also the superscriptions for Psalms 30, 38, 70, and 92. Other superscriptions may give titles of psalm melodies or instruments to be used, for example, "according to the sheminith" in Psalm 6 (compare with Psalms 5, 8, 12, 22, 57, 69, and 77). The technical term *selah,* which appears in many of the psalms, is understood by some to indicate an orchestral interlude or the signal for a silent pause. Fifty-five psalms are entitled "for the director or choir-master."

In the synagogues (prayer or meeting houses), prayer, accompanied by scripture reading and exposition, replaced the sacrificial offerings of the Temple. The rise of the synagogue during the Second Temple period symbolized "the democratization of religion"; the entire community, rather than a priestly elite, was to place every act and moment of life in God's service.[16] Nearly half the psalms were incorporated eventually into the statutory prayers of the synagogue service, including the daily psalms, "which the Levites used to sing in the Temple." The rabbis preached extensively from the psalms, so much so that "there is not a single chapter of Psalms—indeed, hardly a single verse—which is not expounded somewhere in the Talmud and Midrash."[17] In the synagogues, psalms were sung by cantors rather than by Levitical choirs, with the people joining in with chanted refrains. No musical instruments were used.

The New Testament makes it clear that psalms "have been the staple diet of the Church's singing."[18] In 1 Corinthians 14:26, Paul lists the spiritual gifts individual members shared with one another in worship: a hymn (*psalmon*, or psalm), a lesson, a revelation, a tongue, an interpretation. Colossians 3:16–17 urges Christians to teach and admonish each other "as you sing psalms and hymns and spiritual songs with thankfulness in your hearts to God [RSV]"; compare with Ephesians 5:19–20 and Acts 2:42. Tertullian (c. 200 C.E.) affirms the place of the psalms in the Sunday liturgy of the church: "The Scriptures are read and the psalms are sung, sermons are delivered and petitions offered."[19] In the same period, Clement of Alexandria and Origen mention the use of psalms and hymns and the melodies used for them. Psalms were frequently quoted and preached from in the first to fourth centuries, and Jerome even advised women and children to learn Hebrew so that they might be able to read and sing the psalms in their original tongue. Such knowledge was often required for ordination.

The oldest liturgies of the church, both East and West, require at least three lessons: from Hebrew Scripture, Epistles or Acts, and the Gospels. After the Hebrew Scripture lesson, a psalm was sung, and after the Epistle, an Alleluia chant. In the Latin church this psalm came to be known as the Gradual because it was sung from the step *(gradus)* of the pulpit where the lesson was read. As early as the second century, each psalm was followed by the Gloria Patri (glory be to the Father) to show that the psalms were accepted as Christian expressions with specific references to Jesus. The early church used the psalms to help it interpret Christ, and Christ became the interpretative key for unlocking the psalms.

No evidence exists for a fixed schedule of daily lessons and psalms in the liturgies of the early church. The Gradual was chanted by a cantor (a practice taken over from the synagogue), with the congregation and later a choir responding with a refrain. This responsorial model can be seen in the psalms themselves (Psalms 42, 43, 107, and 136). Since liturgical development was slow during the first to the fourth centuries, the music of the Gradual was originally very simple. The melodies of the Gradual were eventually, however, taken over by professional soloists, so that Pope Gregory the Great in 595 assigned the Gradual to lesser ministries; "while search is made for a good voice, no care is taken to provide that the life shall be such as harmonizes with the holy ministry."[20]

After Constantine's conversion to Christianity in 312, when the church enjoyed peace from persecution and support from wealthy benefactors, both the churches and the liturgy became more elaborate. Choirs supplemented congregational responses to cantor melodies, and antiphonal singing (the singing of psalm verses alternately by two groups of singers) developed out of Antioch in the mid-fourth century. This style spread quickly to monastic communities. The use of the antiphon also arose; one or two verses from the psalms would be sung at the beginning and end of the psalm. The seasons of the year determined the choice of antiphon. Changing antiphons could underscore different themes within the same psalm. In addition to the Gradual, three antiphonal psalms in the ancient Roman liturgy (Introit, Offertory, and Communion) functioned as devotional accompaniments to processions within the service.

In the Middle Ages the use of psalms in worship declined radically. Processions were shortened and communion was limited to a few times per year because of a lack of resident clergy, there were few cantors or choirs who could read the Latin of the service and chant the psalms, and books and music were too expensive for most parishes. All the parts of the liturgy were copied in a one-volume Missal, and psalmody was reduced to a few verses read by the priest.

Despite their decline in medieval worship, the psalms had continued to serve as the central focus for the daily devotions of monks in monastic communities since the development of monasticism in the fourth century. The church had taken over this practice of daily prayer from the Jews, who were required to pray twice a day (morning and afternoon), these times corresponding to the *Tamid* sacrifice in the Temple.[21]

By the end of the second century, the church had increased the number of daily prayer times from two (morning and evening) to six. Rather than being tied to times of corporate worship, these Daily Offices were meant to promote reflection on Christ's death and resurrection.[22] Whether the psalms were recited at these times is uncertain. In the monastic communities, East and West, seven Daily Offices were prayed to accord with Psalm 119:164: "Seven times a day I praise you for your righteous judgments." The psalms were distributed so that all 150 were sung once a week, with double offices on major saints' days. Each office was introduced by a dialogue of versicles and responses between the officiant and the others praying.

By the sixteenth century, the seven Daily Offices became too much for priests living outside the monasteries. Many reformers followed Luther, who valued the daily reading of the psalms but cut them back to twice a day, midnight and 6 P.M. (Matins and Vespers), each with three psalms. Psalms within worship enjoyed renewed status, as Calvin argued that "only God's Word was worthy to be sung in God's praise"; he allowed no music in worship except that of the metrical psalms.[23] His Genevan Psalter (1562), with its regular rhythms, was singable by most congregations and did not require trained choirs. English-speaking congregations of the time also sang metrical psalms; no hymns were introduced until the eighteenth century. Given this situation, it is no surprise that the first book printed in the American colonies was the Bay Psalm Book (1640). In many American hymnals, "All People That on Earth Do Dwell," based upon Psalm 100 and sung to the tune of "Old Hundredth," remains as an example of this metrical psalmody.

In the early eighteenth century, Isaac Watts, "the father of

English hymnody," who complained of wretched psalm singing in his church, began to paraphrase, modernize, and christianize the psalms. His hymns, such as "Joy to the World" (based upon Psalm 98), were published in 1707. After Watts's death, it took almost one hundred years for hymn singing to become firmly established in England and America. At any rate, by the end of the eighteenth century, psalms were on their way out as the centerpiece of song in worship.

Today, Roman Catholics in the wake of Vatican II, Lutherans, Episcopalians, and Methodists have all returned to the use of psalms at points in the liturgy in which psalms have been customary. The Presbyterian Church (U.S.A.) is preparing a new hymnal and liturgical psalter. The charismatic movement has been using psalms in worship since the 1960s. The Christian Reformed Church in America still uses psalms for half of its congregational singing. Yet the old pattern of the use of psalms in the Call to Worship and as responsive readings still permeates most Protestant worship services. The recovery of the psalms for our prayer and song in worship is underway but incomplete.

The Development of the Psalter

It is important to keep in mind that the Psalter in its present form is not the result of one single act of collecting by a single person or a group of persons. There was no editor in ancient Israel working feverishly to meet a publisher's deadline and craft a catchy press release. We can see this just by looking at the Psalter itself, which shows traces of growth over a long period of time, probably many centuries.

The Psalter as we have it now is divided into five books, each of which is marked off at the beginning by "Book I," etc. and by a closing doxology (a speaking of praise to God).[24] Book I, for example, includes Psalms 1 through 41. Verse 13 of Psalm 41, which is not a part of the literary whole that is Psalm 41, functions as the closing doxology for Book I: "Blessed be the Lord, the God of Israel, from everlasting to everlasting! Amen and Amen [rsv]." (See also Psalms 72:18–19; 89:52; and 106:48 for the closing doxologies of Books II, III, and IV, respectively.) The whole of

Psalm 150 concludes not only Book V (Psalms 107–149) with doxology but the entire Psalter as well.

This five-fold division is an artificial construct superimposed on various independently circulating collections of psalms. One can think of the Psalter as composed of different little psalters and psalm collections that were in circulation before the book assumed its final form.[25] This view is supported by several clues within the Book of Psalms. For example, in the editorial postcript of Psalm 72, verse 20, which ends Book II, we read: "The prayers of David, the son of Jesse, are ended." Indeed, most of the psalms within Books I and II bear the superscription *"leDavid,"* "a psalm of David." But other "psalms of David" are found, for example, in Book V (Psalms 108–110 and 138–145). This means that only at one stage in the history of the formation of the Psalter, or for one group of worshipers in a particular region, did the psalms of David end there.

That there were separate psalm collections can be supported by the occurrence of doublets in the Psalter; that is, the same psalm or part of a psalm appears twice. Psalm 14 repeats Psalm 53; 40:13–17 is the equivalent of Psalm 70; 57:7–11 plus 60:5–12 repeat Psalm 108. These were probably popular songs that found a place in more than one collection. Also, Psalms 1–41 and 42–83 use different Hebrew terms for deity. The former group uses predominantly the Hebrew Tetragrammaton (four consonants, revealed to Moses at the burning bush), translated in most Bibles as LORD or *Yahweh*. Pious Jews vocalize this as *Adonai*, the practice that I will follow in this book. The Psalm 42–83 collection uses mostly the term *Elohim*, which is translated as *God*.

This so-called Elohistic Psalter may have existed independently before being incorporated into the final collection, as a look at the doublets Psalms 14 and 53 suggests. Psalm 14 uses the divine name Adonai, while Psalm 53 uses Elohim. Smaller collections within the Elohistic Psalter include the psalms of the Asaph guild (50, 73–83), the Korah guild (42–49), and another group of "David" psalms (51–72).

The psalms in each of the five books of the Psalter are not all related to each other in the way that songs are grouped according to theme in our modern hymnals. In fact, a quick reading of all one hundred fifty psalms in order takes one on a roller coaster ride of emotion, from joy to despair, to anger, to thanksgiving, and back again. Though the collection as we have it probably took final shape sometime after the fall of Jerusalem in 587 B.C.E., either in exile in Babylonia or after the return to Judah from exile, many of the psalms within it are quite old and probably were used much earlier in Israel's worship life. In this sense, calling the Psalter "the hymnbook of the Second Temple" is misleading. The Psalter reflects a long history of worship before the Second Temple came into being.

The Septuagint (LXX, the Greek translation of Hebrew Scriptures begun in 250 B.C.E. by the Greek-speaking Jews of Alexandria), which the early church used as its Bible, helps us to set a date before 200 B.C.E. for the final editing of the Book of Psalms, since in the Septuagint we find the collection, by and large, as we have it now. It is also from the Septuagint that we get the word *psalm,* from the Greek *psalmos* which translates the Hebrew term *mizmor.* This term is used in the title or superscription of fifty-seven psalms and means, perhaps, a song accompanied by a stringed instrument. In one Greek manuscript, the whole collection of psalms is called *psalterion,* the term for a harp.

The Septuagint also divides the psalms differently from the Hebrew text. In the Hebrew, Psalms 9 and 10 are two separate psalms, but in the LXX they are combined, as are also Psalms 114 and 115. On the other hand, the LXX splits in two Psalms 116 and 147, whereas they are one in the Hebrew. Consequently, the LXX numbering of Psalms 9–146 does not follow that of the Hebrew text. Confusion also surrounds the numbering of verses *within* a psalm. Some English translations (notably JPS, the Jewish Publication Society), follow the Hebrew numbering by including the superscription (the title written above the psalms) as the first line of the psalm; most others begin verse numbering after the superscription.

Psalm Interpretation

Unlike our modern hymnals, the Book of Psalms does not identify for us the author or date of each psalm. The ancient world was little interested in the question of authorship; no one worried about copyright infringement. We can say nothing concrete about psalm authors; they remain anonymous. Nor do we find any absolutely clear indications of the date of particular psalms, except perhaps for Psalm 137: "By the rivers of Babylon, there we sat down and wept"; here the Babylonian exile in the sixth century B.C.E. seems to be in view.

Psalms were not always treated in this way, however. At the turn of the century, in the early 1900s, scholars tried to match situations depicted in the psalms with particular events in King David's life or in the history of Israel. In this historicizing kind of interpretation, David was considered to be the author of most of the psalms. The fact that seventy-three of the psalms in the Psalter were connected with David through their superscriptions was drawn on to support this view. The superscription of Psalm 41, for example, reads: "To the choirmaster, a psalm *leDavid,*" which most Bibles translate as "a psalm of David." The Hebrew phrase is made up of the preposition *lamed* and the proper name David. This phrase need not suggest authorship, though, as mentioned earlier, it has been traditionally understood as indicating that David composed the psalm. Instead, the fluidity of the Hebrew preposition allows for translations such as "to David," "in the style of David," "in honor of David," or "according to the direction of David."

It was natural for Israel to tie the psalms to David, who enjoyed a great reputation as singer, musician, and poet. David, as the story goes, was introduced into Saul's court for that very reason. "So Saul said to his servants, 'Provide for me a man who can play well, and bring him to me'. . . . And whenever the evil spirit from God was upon Saul, David took the lyre and played it with his hand; so Saul was refreshed, and was well [1 Sam. 16:17, 23, RSV]" (compare with Amos 6:5). It was also David who made Jerusalem the political and religious capital of his kingdom by bringing the Ark of the Covenant into it (2 Samuel 6) and by proposing to build there a permanent house for the Lord (2 Samuel 7). 1 Chronicles, as we have seen above, credits David with organizing the choir guilds and worship of the Temple.

In ancient Israel, the superscription *leDavid* came to mean "belonging to David" or "of David [JPS]," not necessarily in the sense that David authored the psalm, but rather that the community at worship identified itself with this very human king. To strengthen this association with David, later editors of the psalm collection developed biographical notes and attached them to the superscriptions to indicate the historical situation in which David composed or recited the psalm (for example, Psalms 3, 7, 18, 34, 51, 52, 54, 56, 57, 59, 60, 63 and 142).

Thus the superscription of Psalm 51, a penitential lament in which the psalmist begs for God's forgiveness, reads: "A Psalm of David, when Nathan the prophet came to him, after he had gone into Bathsheba [RSV]." This tendency to associate psalms with David continued in the Septuagint. Fifteen more psalms were tagged with leDavid, even Psalm 137! In the New Testament, David was seen as the author of psalms (see Mark 12:35–37; Acts 4:25–26; and Romans 4:6–8).

Patrick Miller points out that superscriptions like that in Psalm 51 can give us some clues about how the psalm was understood in ancient Israel. Superscriptions "are a way of saying that the psalms over which the superscription is written make sense in just such a context."[26] A variety of human experiences that come forth from the biblical story can also provide a context for a psalm's meaning; we need not be tied to the search for only one explanation. Thus, David's sin with Bathsheba is one way, not the way, of understanding Psalm 51.

David was not the only focus of those who wanted to historicize the psalms. Some scholars moved in the opposite direction historically and argued that the Psalter was "the hymnbook of the Second Temple," and, as such, its psalms were composed late in Israel's history, in the period after the return from exile in 538 B.C.E. Others argued for the Maccabean period because the psalms articulated the personal experience of pious Jews who were persecuted by the "godless," a situation that fits with the oppression of the Jews by Seleucid rulers in the second century B.C.E. This oppression led to a revolt by the Maccabees, a priestly family who won independence from the Seleucids for the Jews.

These scholars held a very negative view of Israelite worship; such personal piety and individual relationship with God could not be preexilic or part of Second Temple worship. They concluded that such piety could only emerge when worship was freed from formality and the Temple.[27] This kind of reasoning has helped to drive a wedge of discontinuity between Second Temple Judaism and early Christianity, and has fueled the fires of antiJudaism throughout the church's history.

The problem is that all of these arguments for dating the psalms are very general. There is simply not enough information within the psalms themselves to date most psalms accurately. This problem was addressed by Hermann Gunkel in the 1920s in his form-critical focus upon psalm types rather than upon authors and their personal experiences. For Gunkel, since the psalms originated in typical worship situations, the question of authorship was unimportant; in worship, the psalms become the property of all worshipers. Gunkel identified several distinctive literary psalm types, among them, the hymn, the lament, the thanksgiving, and the royal psalm; each type had its own special form and content growing out of a distinctive setting in life in which that psalm type functioned. A lament, for example, may have been prayed in the Temple when enemies defeated Israel in battle or prayed at home when illness struck a family; a thanksgiving may have been offered up after a good harvest or recovery from sickness. In this sense a psalm cannot be pinned down to one particular time in Israel's history or associated with one particular person and can be more readily appropriated by worshipers of any time and place.

We exercise form-critical judgments whenever we write letters or read the newspaper. We do not normally send a business letter to a best friend telling about the birth of our first baby, nor do we send a friendly letter to the bank requesting a loan. We do not usually read an editorial in the same way that we read a news article. The expectations connected with each situation govern the form and content of our communication in that situation. Our modern church hymnals also illustrate this form-critical method. Hymns are usually grouped under headings like "Praise of God," "The Church," "Jesus Christ," "The Holy Spirit," "Discipleship," etc. and also according to their place in the worship service or the liturgical seasons of the church year.

Ironically, form criticism in the hands of Gunkel's followers Sigmund Mowinckel and Artur Weiser became somewhat of an obstacle to the modern reappropriation of the psalms. These scholars focused upon one liturgical setting that they saw dominating Israel's worship life as the situation out of which most of the psalms arose. They both tried to explain too much from one reconstructed festival, itself built on shaky comparative data and too many general truths.[28] For Mowinckel, the liturgical setting was that of the annual enthronement festival of Adonai, celebrated in the Jerusalem Temple during the New Year celebration in the fall. For Weiser, it was the covenant renewal festival celebrated in connection with the Feast of Booths in the fall.

Since Christians do not celebrate such festivals, how could they understand how these psalms, which grew out of these festivals, really functioned and what these psalms really meant? Also, the psalms seemed to be removed from daily faith struggles; after all, sometimes the one offering the thanksgiving shout in winter cannot wait to offer it up to God during the festival celebration the following fall! And was there room for lament at all when the festival emphasis was upon celebration?

Fortunately, out of these questions came new approaches to the psalms that focused upon the dynamics of faith within them rather than upon their liturgical settings. Claus Westermann argues that there are two basic psalm categories, praise and lament. The setting in life of the psalms is unimportant, because praise and lament are the two "basic modes of thought when [humans] turn to God with words."[29] These two categories reflect our human movement between lament and praise on the continuum of prayer. The movement within the lament psalms from alienation to praise and thanksgiving also expresses this dynamic of the God/human encounter.

Brueggemann builds on Westermann and focuses on the function or "social usefulness" of the psalms. It is not enough, he argues, to say that the function of a lament is to lament. Instead, we must ask how the psalms function as voices of faith in the life of a community of believers. To answer this question, he rearranges the form-critical categories of psalm type according to the themes, or "seasons of life," they express, the seasons of *orientation*, *disorientation*, and *new orientation*.[30]

Orientation is a season of well-being, order, security, and trust in the reliability of God's good creation. Psalm hymns to God as Creator, hymns to the God of Zion, wisdom psalms, and Torah psalms articulate the orientation of this no-surprise world.

Disorientation is a season of disorder, suffering, and alienation. Psalm laments bring this pain of shattered order to expression.

New orientation is a season in which a surprising new gift from the sovereign God is received just when one was not expected. Thanksgiving psalms and hymns to God the sovereign (the so-called enthronement psalms) articulate this season of life.

The life of faith expressed in the psalms shows two important movements: the move out of orientation to disorientation and the move out of disorientation into new orientation. When something happens to shatter our orientation, such as the death of a loved one, a divorce, or the loss of a job, we tumble into the pit of disorientation, the order of our known world destroyed. This move is accompanied by a rush of what society terms "negative" emotions: anger, resentment, guilt, shame, isolation, grief, despair, hatred, denial. Laments can help us as individuals or as a group to bring this new, painful situation to speech and acknowledge the reality of the experience.

The other move we make is out of disorientation to new orientation. This move is accompanied by a rush of "positive" emotions: surprise, gratitude, delight, wonder, awe. Thanksgiving psalms and enthronement hymns tell of God's rescue, deliverance, healing, and reversal of the situation of distress. For Christians, the first move is embodied in the crucifixion of Jesus; the second, in his resurrection.

Brueggemann argues that we are regularly surprised by and resistant to these movements of faith. Think about that the next time you ask someone, "How are you?" Do you really want to know, or has this become just another social greeting? How comfortable would you be if someone responded by telling you exactly how he or she felt, either miserable in the pit of disorientation or wonderingly thankful in her or his new orientation, with all the corresponding details! You would probably hurry off with some excuse, eager to get away from someone like that!

Chapter 2

Your Hallelujahs Don't Have to Be Hollow Anymore

Psalm Hymns

The Hebrew title of the Psalter is *tehillim*, "praises," from the Hebrew root *hillel*. Our English word *hallelujah* is a transliteration of the Hebrew word, which can be broken down into two parts: *hallelu*, a command meaning "praise!" and *jah*, the German spelling for the shortened *Yah* of the divine name Yahweh, Israel's special name for God (Adonai, LORD). Whenever we say "hallelujah!" in worship we are speaking Hebrew! Hallelujah means literally "praise Yahweh," or "praise the LORD," or "praise Adonai." Remember, nearly one-third of Hebrew Scripture is in poetic form; other "praises" outside the Book of Psalms are the Song of the Sea in Exodus 15:1–18, the Song of Deborah in Judges 5:1–31, the Song of Hannah in 1 Samuel 2:1–10, hymns in Isaiah, and laments in Jeremiah.

Calling the whole psalm collection "praises" means that Israel considered everything in the psalms—even the laments as well as the hymns, thanksgivings, and wisdom psalms—to be praise of God. This inclusive sense of praise can help Christian liturgy, that is, "the public worship of the Church," to retain its meaning as "the work of the people," in the sense that Geoffrey Wainwright intends. Wainwright argues that "into the liturgy the people bring their entire existence so that it may be gathered up in praise"[1];

from the liturgy they depart with a "renewed vision" of God's realm. Since the psalms articulate the varied experiences of human existence, they provide ready vehicles for our liturgy, for the gathering up of our lives in praise. Our liturgy, then, ought to embrace the full range of psalm prayer as "praises."

A hymn is specifically in the form-critical sense a song of praise to God. Hymns were identified by Hermann Gunkel as a psalm literary type with a special form and content. There are several subgroups of hymns—hymns to God as Creator of the world (Psalms 8, 33, 104, 145, 148) and of Israel as a nation (95, 105, 114, 135, 136), hymns to the God of Zion (46, 48, 84, 87, 122), and hymns to God the Sovereign (29, 47, 93, 96–99, the so-called enthronement psalms)—each subgroup emphasizing a particular characteristic, or aspect, of God in praise.

In this chapter we will consider in detail Psalms 150, 104, and 46. Psalm 150 cannot readily be classified as one of the subgroups of hymns. It is a great summary hymn, a psalm of praise for the entire Book of Psalms, and gives us a glimpse of how powerful (and noisy!) our praise can be. Psalm 104 is an example of a hymn to God as Creator, which reminds us of God's continuing creative activity in the world. As a hymn to the God of Zion, Psalm 46 presents us with a picture of the future that God intends for us, a picture that judges our present.

Brueggemann argues that hymns to God the Creator express the faith theme of orientation, that is, of security, well-being, and trust in God's order, while hymns to God the Sovereign articulate new orientation, or the surprise of a new situation when one's orderly world has fallen apart. In this way, Brueggemann's themes of the life of faith cut across form-critical lines, bringing together "the gains of critical study . . . and the realities of human life."[2]

Because the themes of our faith journey guide this book, hymns to God the Sovereign will not be discussed until chapter 6, with other psalms of new orientation. When classifying a psalm, remember that there exists no master computer printout making clear which psalms belong to which theme or form-critical category. The same psalm may express more than one theme, depending upon the intention of its speaker and the use to which it is put.

The Function of Praise

What is it that we do when we praise God in a psalm hymn? How does our praise function? We cannot answer these questions by merely asserting that the content of the psalm hymn is praise and that the function of the hymn form is to articulate praise of God in a situation that calls for such praise. That would be the traditional form-critical answer, which focuses upon the theological function of the psalms. Consider instead this comment: "Often, in listening to the prayers presented publicly in churches, it seems as if the form of praise is merely a preamble—a suitable introduction to the real business of asking for things which are bound to follow!"[3]

In this connection, think about how our Sunday liturgies are constructed. We usually begin with a call to worship that praises God (often in the form of an excerpt from or pastiche of psalms), followed by a song from our hymnals praising God, followed by confession of sin and then the assurance of pardon. Only then can we hear the scripture lessons read and proclaimed and raise our petitionary and intercessory prayers. It does seem that praise functions as a preamble for the real business of asking for things! Is our praise of God in worship simply a tool for buttering up God, a means to an end? Have we become so mechanical and unthinking in our praise that our hallelujahs have become hollow?

A study of psalm hymns can show us just how unbiblical our hollow hallelujahs are. In praising, Israel learned about God and was given a model for its response to God. As psalm scholar Patrick Miller puts it: "Praise is language to God and about God, elicited out of the human experience of God."[4] In praise we learn about God as well as about ourselves and our place in the world. In praise we both acknowledge the infinite possibilities that God has set before us as well as confess our dependence upon God who created us. It is this discovery and acknowledgment of who we are as dependent creatures of the Creator that is, I think, especially missing in our hollow hallelujahs. As Bruce Birch argues, "Much of our worship in the U.S. churches . . . has been lacking in any sense of recognition of dependency on God. The church has been affected by our national ideal of self-sufficiency. Thus, many worship services speak more of self-congratulation than of praise."[5]

The community of faith exists to praise God. This is part of Second Isaiah's message to the community of exiles: "I will make a way in the wilderness and rivers in the desert . . . to give drink to my chosen people, the people whom I formed for myself that they might declare my praise [Isa. 43:19b, 20b, 21, rsv]." This praise of the faith community is humbled when it joins with the praise of the whole created order: "Praise Adonai, sun and moon, praise Adonai, all you stars of light! Praise Adonai you heights of heaven [Ps. 148:3, 4a]!"

Some psalm laments use this recognition of the creature's duty to praise the Creator as a motivation for God to act to end the present distress; if the psalmist dies, praise of God will come to an end. One's inability to praise is God's loss; "the speaker is *valued by God as one who praises.*"6 For example, Psalm 30:9 pleads: "What profit is there in my death, if I go down to the Pit? Can dust praise you? Can it declare your faithfulness?" (compare with Psalms 6:5; 9:13–14; 88:10).

Vows of praise in psalm laments function similarly in their anticipation of the deliverance that has not yet occurred. The psalmist pledges "I will sing praise to the name of Adonai, the Most High [Ps. 7:17]" with the understanding, I will do this *if* you deliver me (compare with 13:6; 22:22; 26:12; 35:28; 71:16, 22–24). Here we have the idea that the psalmist acts through praise as God's "public relations agent" in the world.

Our praises then can help us to define ourselves in the world; they can influence our self-identification. As Bruce Birch suggests, praise marks us as the people of God in that our offering of praise is an acknowledgment of dependency on God, an act of community, and a reminder of the power of symbols especially in a time of crisis.7 In praise we know who and whose we are; we know humility. We are reminded that our relationship with God is not private, but a shared experience with the people of God of all times. Amidst confusion and crisis, the praise of God in worship provides a focused center that demands the recovery of our historic symbols and language. In and through praise, then, we can become fully human, fully whole, and firmly anchored in community.

Further, this praise of ours is never static; instead, it speaks of our dynamic relationship with God. It makes sense, then, that

Claus Westermann views responsive praise to God as one pole along the continuum of prayer between supplication and praise.[8] Miller argues that rather than swinging back and forth like a pendulum between supplication and praise, one is always "moving *toward* praise . . . Praise and thanks are in a sense the *final* word, the direction one is headed, in the relationship with God."[9] Thus, although we may begin our worship services with praise, praise is also the final goal of worship. The New Testament articulates this movement toward praise in Philippians 2:10–11: ". . . that at the name of Jesus every knee should bow . . . and every tongue confess that Jesus Christ is Lord [RSV]." A later confessional understanding of this goal is found in the first question of the Westminster Shorter Catechism: What is the chief end of human life? "to glorify God and enjoy [God] forever."

The Psalter shows this movement toward praise, not only within individual psalms, but throughout the whole collection. More laments are found in the first half of the Psalter; more hymns in the second half. One cannot trace this movement along a straight line, but "the shift of emphasis is noticeable. To go through the Book of Psalms is to be led increasingly toward the praise of God as the final word."[10]

This shift in emphasis from petition to praise can also be seen outside the Book of Psalms in the Exodus 1–15 story of slavery overturned by God, in Hannah's lament over barrenness turned to thanksgiving for the God who gives her a child (1 Samuel 1–2), and in the praise of the Creator who is about to create anew and bring comfort to the Israelites in exile in Isaiah 40–55.[11] It is this experience of and response to the God of reversals that erupts into praise. Thus we can see that "the praise of God in the Old Testament is always devotion that tells about God, that is, **theology,** and proclamation that seeks to draw others into the circle of those who worship this God, that is, **testimony for conversion.**"[12] The New Testament call to discipleship embraces these elements of devotion and proclamation found in Hebrew Scripture.

Dare we open our mouths with hollow hallelujahs when so much is at stake? We are no less than theologians when we take up a psalm of praise as our own, no less than missionaries when we testify to our experience of God in the praise that we offer. We take our stand within the community of the faithful, beckoning others to join us because of who God is and what God has done. Our praise underscores the universal in its acknowledgment of our shared experiences.

There is another aspect of our praise that we must consider. Brueggemann argues that a hymn of praise is an articulation of orientation that affirms a well-ordered, no-surprise, reliable world. As such, it is an expression of creation faith; trust in God's order emerges from the daily workings of the world and leads to an affirmation of God's faithfulness. Such hymns give testimony to and proclaim the nature of God. They say simply that "this is the way things are" rather than "this is what happened."

Hymn praise can function in two ways sociologically, one positive and one negative. First, it can create and keep in place a "sacred canopy." This kind of hymn praise celebrates a relied upon givenness guaranteed by God, "under which the community of faith can live out its life with freedom from anxiety."[13] Brueggemann warns us, however, that we must ask who experiences life as ordered, reliable, and good? Who wants to make these kind of assertions, and why? One could say that it is the well-off, the economically secure, and the powerful who experience life as ordered and good. If these secure ones pray hymns of praise, they convert no one, because they testify to oriented persons like themselves who celebrate the status quo. This is the negative dimension of hymn praise. Creation faith expressed in hymn praise can grant self-approval and serve "as a form of social control." We must watch for "the slippery ways in which creation faith easily becomes social conservatism, which basks in our own well-off-ness."[14]

The church will be a "speaker of orientation" in the negative sense through its psalms of praise unless it acknowledges that not everyone experiences life as good and ordered and that orientation for some comes at the expense of others. A quick look at the television or the newspaper ought to confirm this. "The fact is: the world is not an easy place in which to live doxologically."[15] We must ask if our own praise embraces the pain of the world and its injustice or ignores it. Do we view those who are not secure and well off as outside God's creation blessing? Do we undergird structures of injustice with our status quo praise that keeps the powerless in line?

If we do, then we need to recognize and affirm a second sociological function for hymns of praise, one that focuses upon the eschatological nature of praise. Wainwright speaks of the "eschatological tension" that marks Christian living and is focused in Christian ritual. This tension marks the church as it is in the world, a "pilgrim community," struggling to become the church as it is meant to be, the people of God's final realm. Christian rituals do not usually maintain a once-given world order but are "predominantly transformative in character," helping to shape the church into what it is to become.[16]

In the same way, this tension can be found within psalm hymns of praise in that they anticipate an ordered and oriented life that is not yet experienced. Psalm hymns point to God's good purposes and intention for the world, to creation that is not yet completed. With this eschatological reading, psalm hymns can give hope to the oppressed, for order is lifted up as God's intention for *all* creation, and we are tapped as cocreators with God of that order-in-the-making. If we are aware of how we use a psalm hymn, we can promote social criticism and transformation instead of social control.[17]

It is in fact to the transforming eschatological element in American black worship that James Cone points as a source of the radical change in black identity. In worship, blacks see "a new vision of their future humanity. . . . they are no longer named by the world but named by the Spirit of Jesus." This is a liberating experience, which defines blacks anew in the face of their humiliation and oppression by white social and religious structures. "It is this experience of being radically transformed by the power of the Spirit that defines the primary style of black worship."[18]

Brueggemann argues that though ancient Israel's praise grew out of its experiences of rescue and transformation by God, this praise became distorted as it was linked closely with the royal palace and the Temple complex. Praise came to serve the interests of the king and those in control, legitimating the royal social system. This was idolatrous praise. In order to recover its genuine praise, Israel had to return again and again to its concrete memories and experiences of transformation that overturned such distortions.[19] In the same way today, the church as a speaker of orientation needs to turn to its concrete and transforming memories in order to overcome its distortions and recapture genuine praise. Lifting up the eschatological element in psalm hymns can help the church in its crucial task of becoming inclusive, that is, of embracing all persons as the body of Christ in the world.

The Structure of the Hymn Psalm

Both the form and content of the hymn of praise in the Psalter bear witness to Israel's experience of God. They also invite us to join in the praise. Hymns usually unfold in three parts: (1) the summons to praise, (2) the motive or reason for praise, and (3) the closing call to praise. The summons to praise is normally a plural command; the plural suggests a setting within communal worship. We are thus reminded by the hymn language that praise is not a private matter. We call others to hear what we have to say about God, and we ought, therefore, to give careful and earnest voice to our words.

One of the oldest hymns in Hebrew Scripture, the Song of Miriam in Exodus 15:21, begins with the plural command "Sing to Adonai" and is followed by the reason for this summons: "for [because] Adonai has triumphed gloriously; the horse and his rider [Adonai] has thrown into the sea." There is no closing summons, which is true of several psalm hymns. The opening summons to sing is thus connected in the Song of Miriam with Israel's experience of deliverance by Adonai in the Exodus. The praise is real and joyous.

Patrick Miller suggests that though this praise may even be exuberant, it is "never irrational, . . . To the contrary, praise is a making glad that makes sense."[20] This is the case even when Israel is called to praise God in a general way for God's majesty or creative power, instead of for a concrete act of deliverance as, for example, in Psalms 104 or 148. Often the active participle "one who does . . ." communicates God's majesty or creative power; the participle suggests the general nature and activity of God, God's ongoing processes, what God does regularly and everywhere, rather than "an intrusive eventfulness."[21]

Miller suggests that one acknowledges God's glory in this general way as one acknowledges the beauty of a flower.[22] In fleshing out his analogy, I imagine myself on a walk alongside a stream when I discover an exquisite wildflower nestled among the rocks. As soon as I see it, before I can think about why it is beautiful, I suck in my breath with an "oh!" of wonder and appreciation, simply because I have encountered it. In the same way, praise of God is, as Miller puts it, "unavoidable" simply because God is, simply because of our relationship with God. In this light, one could say that the opening summons of the three-part hymn structure is prereflective, pretheological in mood.

The body of the hymn giving the motive for praise would be analogous to my lingering to consider the color of the flower, the arrangement of its petals, the shape of its leaves, the way the sunlight plays upon it. The flower has not actively done anything, but I consider why it is beautiful. My consideration of its beauty is analogous to the body of the hymn, which is a deliberate theological effort. The closing summons to praise would be built upon my examination of the flower and would be a "making glad that makes sense."

Psalm 117 offers a compact example of the hymn structure. Verse 1 erupts with "Hallelujah [praise Adonai] all nations! Extol Adonai, all peoples!" This sweeping summons to praise is followed by the reason for praise, customarily introduced by the Hebrew particle *kî* ("because," or "for"). Why are nations and peoples called to praise Adonai? "For [because] great is Adonai's *ḥesed* towards us, and the reliability of Adonai is forever." *Ḥesed* is usually translated as "lovingkindness" or "steadfast love" but also speaks directly of God's covenant loyalty. Because God's faithfulness in covenant has been experienced in Israel's past, God's faithfulness can be counted on in Israel's future.[23] Note how God is referred to in the third person; this praise motive tells about God rather than addresses God. The closing "Hallelujah!" illustrates how often the opening call to praise is repeated (compare Psalms 104–106, 113, 115, and 116 with the same ending).

Sometimes the summons to praise is not directed to others. In Psalm 103:1, for example, the self is addressed, but others are also encouraged by this address: "Bless Adonai, O my self, and all my

being, Adonai's holy name!" (compare with Psalm 146:1). In
Psalm 145:1 the psalmist declares: "I will extol you my God and
Sovereign and bless your name forever!" The plural in Psalm 95:1
urges "O come let us sing to Adonai!" In 118:2, after the opening
command comes "Let Israel say 'Adonai's ḥesed endures forever!'"
Sometimes a simple declaration is voiced: "The heavens are telling
the glory of God [Ps. 19:1]" and "Great is Adonai and greatly to be
praised [Ps. 48:1]."

Not only are nations addressed and the psalmist encouraged by
the summons to praise, but often all of creation is called to praise
God, the Creator. "Make a joyful noise to God, all the earth [Ps.
66:1]!"; "Praise Adonai, all the angels! Praise Adonai, all the host
[Ps. 148:2]!"; compare with Psalm 29. Here we see that the
language of praise "is truly primal and universal. All existence is
capable of praising God and does so."[24] This humbling perspective
reminds us that the whole cosmos depends upon this Creator God,
and that the whole cosmos is united in this dependence.

Psalm 33 summons Israel to praise its Creator with five commands: rejoice, praise, make melody, sing, play. The reason for
this "new song" is given in the body, verses 4–19: "For the word of
Adonai is upright and all Adonai's work is done in faithfulness.
The one who loves righteousness and justice, the ḥesed of Adonai
fills the earth." As Miller argues, that word and work is not God's
act of deliverance but the creation of the universe in verses 6–7:
"By the word of Adonai the heavens were made." The beginning of
God's faithful love and justice is creation.[25] The concluding
declaration in verses 20–22 lifts up God's faithful care (ḥesed) as
the ground of Israel's trust and hope. Those who are not able to
"read creation" as Brueggemann puts it, who are not able to see in
its order the loyalty of God, will not be able to trust; they will lead
hopeless lives. Unless one is obedient (the "upright" and "righteous" of verse 1), one "may look and never see. Even creation is
rightly read only through covenantal response, discerned through
believing eyes."[26]

Hymns of praise lift up God the Creator of heaven and earth,
who is also the God of history. Israel offered praise for the story, or
history, of God's mighty deeds on its behalf, as in narrative Psalms
78, 105, 106, 135, and 136. All these deeds of God testify to

God's ongoing faithfulness. The story told in these psalms "is not related with detachment but is told as a drama that is true 'for me' or 'for us'"[27] in the same way that the Christian story is told; Christians incorporate Israel's story of deliverance out of which emerges the story of Jesus Christ.

Psalm 136 forges a clear link between creation and Israel's story in history by tracing God's mighty deeds all the way back to primordial creation. In a litany of praise set in motion by the opening verse, "O give thanks to Adonai, for Adonai is good, for Adonai's ḥesed endures forever," Israel praises God, whose first act was the making of the heavens and the earth and who brought Israel out from Egypt, led them through the wilderness, and settled them in the land. Just as God created the heavens and the earth, God created Israel "out of the historical nothingness of slavery and gave them a future and a vocation."[28] Thus Psalm 100:3 declares: "Know that it is Adonai who is God; God made us and we are God's; we are God's people and sheep of God's pasture"; compare with Psalm 95:6–7.

These hymns of narrative praise of the God of history prompt us to look for evidence of God at work in our history. Where do we see signs of God's concrete action in the world today, action that elicits our praise? Perhaps God's loyal action on our behalf can be seen in the amazing turn to democracy of East Germany and other peoples in eastern Europe; the Berlin Wall has been dismantled, and the two Germanies work toward reunification. The freeing of Nelson Mandela from a South African prison after twenty-eight years of confinement also evidences God's work in the world; the African National Congress (ANC) and the government of South Africa are talking to one another! The Soviet Union allows Christians to worship and criticism of the government to be voiced; the "evil empire" presents us with a much different face. God is at work in our world, overcoming the barriers that divide peoples from one another.

We can also ask how God is at work closer to home, in the United States. The pro-choice and anti-abortion supporters who organized various marches on Washington, advocates of the home-less, people against drug abuse, and other groups all witness to God's work here in America. Local churches throughout America act as the instruments of God's work through the homeless shelters and day-care centers they operate, through Alcoholics Anonymous, Cub Scouts, and other groups that are invited to use their buildings, through the lobbying they do for affordable housing in their communities.

It may be difficult for us to acknowledge that these all are ways in which God is working through us to shape the world into what God intends. Sometimes we prefer to limit God to spiritual activity; God comes to us during Sunday worship, we say hello, and then we go about business as usual for the rest of the week. Church becomes in this way an escape from the world and its problems rather than an embrace of the world; Sunday liturgy no longer functions as "the work of the people." Jesus' life and ministry, however, calls us to confront the reality of the world. Jesus lived among us on earth and took our problems upon himself; he is "the Word made flesh." If we are to be the body of Christ in the world, then we must stop resisting seeing God at work in certain actions and people.

We might prefer a God we can control and be comfortable with rather than a God who challenges us. We would like to say "God is on my side, not yours," but such a God would not be the Creator of the world and all its people. Such a God would be our personal puppet. Perhaps we restrict God in this way because we think that we are in control, that we are the center of life. We do not want to give up our power and acknowledge that all of our life is a gift from God the Creator. Perhaps we resist because we are afraid, afraid of the changes that must come when we give ourselves and our world over to the God who made us and who controls history.

If we took seriously the words of Psalm 100, "It is Adonai who made us, and we are Adonai's. We are God's people, and the sheep of God's pasture," we would reflect God's character in the way we live our lives as God's creatures. We would perhaps more readily offer ourselves as instruments for God's work in the world and more readily recognize God at work in the world through one another. In this way our praise of God would become a shared praise and not our private undertaking. We would learn how to listen to the praise of others whose experiences are different from ours. We would come to see that there is no national or economic or cultural litmus test for praise of the Creator of us all. To claim membership in God's people would mean that we acknowledge our mutual dependence upon God and our unity in that dependence.

Psalm 150: "The Great Hallelujah"

Psalm 150 is often called "The Final Hallelujah" or "The Great Hallelujah," because it offers a fitting general doxology for the end of the Psalter. The opening imperative call to praise in verse 1 begins with "hallelujah!" Praise is to come from God's sanctuary, or holy place, and from God's mighty firmament. What is suggested by these words in verse 1 is that praise unites two spheres of the cosmos: heaven (God's mighty firmament) and earth (God's sanctuary). The whole creation is one in praise of the Creator. As Artur Weiser argues: "In praising God, the meaning of the world is fulfilled. To praise the abundance of God's power is the purpose which links together the most diverse voices in heaven and on earth in a tremendous symphonic hymn of praise."[29]

The shortest section of this hymn is the body in verse 2. The motive for praise is not introduced by "because" or an active participle; we are simply called to praise God for mighty deeds and exceeding greatness. The closing, verses 3–6, constitutes a renewed and expanded call to praise. The stress is on how one is to praise, with the entire temple orchestra: with trumpet, lute, harp, timbrel (like a tambourine), dance, strings, pipe, cymbals (loud, clashing cymbals). Everything that breathes must praise God.

Two observations emerge out of this structure. First of all, and quite obviously, Psalm 150 reminds us that Israel's praise was not always subdued or reflective but sometimes raucous and exuberant. The "joyful noise" of Psalm 150 recalls the Song of Miriam in Exodus 15:21 and the dance of the rejoicing women. Worship can involve the whole person—mind, body, and heart—as the Israelites experienced and exemplified. The black church tradition is more comfortable with this kind of praise than many white, mainline churches, which hustle children off to Sunday school sometime during the Scripture reading, whisk crying babies hurriedly out of the sanctuary, resist sacred dance as somehow not dignified enough, and generally show discomfort with praise shouts punctuating sermons or bodies swaying to hymn music. The black embrace of what might be called *becoming* rather than *being* welcomes the joyful noise; perhaps it is the mainline embrace of *being* rather than *becoming* that shuns it.

A second observation about the hymn's structure is that the truncated body of the hymn forces us to look twice at the nature of praise. Most scholars explain the fact that the motive for praise in Psalm 150 is the shortest part of the psalm by pointing to its placement at the end of the collection; all the preceding psalms have given every possible reason for praising God, so no repetition is necessary. Such reasoning underscores the point that hymn praise is solely a response to God, that is, one must praise God because of what God is or has done.

Artur Weiser is representative of this view. For Weiser, the-ophany, or the appearance of God, is the centerpiece of the covenant renewal festival to which psalm hymns are tied. The hymn is thus "a reflex, an echo; it is the Amen of the congregation following the divine self-revelation."[30] A hymn proclaims this theophany to the world through the recitation of God's mighty deeds.

I see in the hymn, however, more than a straight line between divine act and human response within this narrow setting of a festival. The older view of the setting of the psalms in a specific liturgical moment or festival in Israel's worship, as restated by Weiser, draws narrow parameters around the function of praise. The situation is more circular, more dialogical. The relative silence of Psalm 150 regarding the motive of praise points to this circular situation. When God is praised, and praised properly, God is the better for it. God's power becomes more focused; God's power is magnified because God allows and equips the entire universe to sing the divine praises. We praise, not just for the sake of spreading God's name among the world and among ourselves, but for God's sake as well. If our praise makes a difference for the world, then it also makes a difference for God. Those related in worship, God, human beings, and the rest of creation, are all now different from before this worship of praise.

As mentioned earlier, the lamenting psalmists knew this when they reminded God of the "public relations" value of their praise. This view of praise points to the power of worship. All comes from

God; we use God's power to sing God's praises; and all goes back to God. Pentecostals glimpse the power of their praise at the point in their service when they announce, "Now let us minister to the LORD." How does a community of faith minister to God? Through its praise. The hymn titled "Stand up and Bless the Lord," in the new Methodist Hymnal, reflects the same understanding in its first stanza: "Stand up and *bless* the Lord, ye people of [God's] choice; stand up and *bless* the Lord your God with heart and soul and voice" (italics mine). In stanza 2, however, the hymn pulls back from asserting that blessing, or praise, has any power over God, for God is "high above all praise, above all blessing high."

Psalm 150 prompts us to take a careful look at our own praise. If our hallelujahs are hollow it is perhaps because we go through the motions of praise without realizing how much is at stake for us and for God. Perhaps we are unwilling to see God at work concretely in the world and to praise and help in that work. Perhaps we fear throwing our whole selves into worship and revealing too much about ourselves and our dependence upon God. We could avoid hollow hallelujahs if we dared to acknowledge the power of our praise in worship. Praise as an expression of our relationship with God would not allow us simply to butter God up so we could ask for things or to limit the praiseworthy actions of God to the familiar and comfortable. Praise emerging from the circle of relationship that embraces God, human beings, and the created order is praise that can make new, unify, create, and empower. This kind of praise is not tired or routine; it almost bursts out of us. It testifies about God in the presence of other people and focuses God's power. This kind of praise puts us in right relationship with others and with God. It is powerful, indeed.

Psalm 104: A Hymn to God the Creator

Psalm 104 is a hymn to God the Creator. Other psalms in this form-critical category are 8, 19, 29, 33, and 148. Psalm 104 is related in form and content to the Egyptian "Hymn to the Aton." This hymn was discovered in a tomb at el-Amarna, the capital of the Egyptian pharaoh Akhenaton (Amenhotep IV, 1380–1362 B.C.E.), who worshiped the universal care and recreating power of the sun disk (the Aton).[31] This hymn probably came to Israel through wisdom circles (see chapter 3 on wisdom psalms).

The opening summons to praise in Psalm 104 is directed to the self: "Bless Adonai, O my being!" The Hebrew word *nephesh* is translated "being"; it does not mean "soul" in the Christian sense, as it is often translated. In Israelite thought there is no dualism of body and soul, of an indestructible core of being that can be distinguished from physical life. One does not have a *nephesh* but is a *nephesh*. In Psalm 104, the psalmist calls upon his or her whole person, or self, to praise God. Do we throw our whole selves into our praise of God, or are we tepid and timid? The opening of Psalm 104 can serve to remind us not to hold anything back in our praise of God.

The reasons for this self-encouragement to bless are given in the body of the hymn, beginning in verse 1b and continuing through verse 30. The psalmist addresses God directly, using the second person, "you," rather than the customary third person: "O Adonai my God, you are very great. You are clothed with honor and majesty." Following this is a series of descriptive phrases that underscore God's continuous activity in creation as the maintainer of world order: "The one who covers yourself with light as with a garment, who stretches out the heavens like a tent, who sets the beams of [God's] chambers on the waters, who makes the clouds [God's] chariot."

Anderson suggests that the body unfolds in seven sections that follow the sequence of the Genesis 1 creation story.[32] The closing, verses 31–35, returns to the initial theme of God's power. The psalmist prays that God's power may "endure forever" and vows to praise "while I have being." Verse 35c repeats exactly the opening call to praise. The verb *'asah*, which means "to do, make, create," ties the hymn together, since it occurs at the beginning and end of succinct sections of the psalm: verses 4, 13, 19, 24 (twice), and 31; this distribution lifts up God as creator and sustainer of the world.[33]

In verses 1b–4, God's power is described in the language of theophany, that is, God appears in the world in terms of the storm imagery used for ancient Near Eastern storm deities: clouds, wind, fire, and flame. God is not equated with the wind or the clouds or the fire, however; these are God's creations rather than personifications of God. The clouds and wind are God's winged chariot; fire and flame are God's ministers. In the same way God came down to the people at Mt. Sinai to enter into covenant with them: "There were thunders and lightnings, and a thick cloud upon the mountain . . . And all of Mt. Sinai was in smoke, because Adonai descended upon it in fire [Exod. 19:16, 18]."

God's first act, creation, is treated in verses 5–9, a section that calls to mind Genesis 1, Job 38, and Psalm 77:16. Having a narrative of the world's origin and continued existence is one of the characteristics common to the religions of Israel and its neighbors in the ancient Near East.[34] Such narratives that express a world view of a people are called myths. The word *myth* does not characterize a narrative as untrue. A myth is not history, strictly speaking, but myths do portray a people's understanding of their identity and origins as well as those of their gods. One function of myth is to personify the forces and tensions of life and name them; thus, one could praise and petition them for control.

In Psalm 104:5–9, Israel returns to primordial time, to the first act, creation, when Adonai imposed order upon chaos. For Israel the chaos is represented by "the deep" (*tehom*), verse 6.[35] In many myths of creation, water is seen as an enemy, as flood. Water could, through inundation (and also through drought-causing withdrawal) reduce order and life to chaos and death. In verse 7, God "rebukes" the waters and they flee; God's voice is like "thunder." This reference to God's voice draws out the association with "God said" in Genesis 1, creation by the word.

In verse 9, God sets for the waters "a boundary which they should not pass, so that they might not again cover the earth." The "boundary" is the firmament in the heavens, literally, the hammered out part, or dome, in which are slits to allow the chaos waters to fall beneficently to earth as rain. Here the psalmist asserts that the order of the world will endure, that it is not subject to disorder. This is meant to evoke our trust and the no-surprise world of orientation.

The picture of the cosmos in verses 5–9 as a three-tiered universe also supports the assertion of orientation. Earth is a kind of circular disk floating on the ocean, anchored by pillars: "You set earth on its foundations, so that it should never be shaken or totter [v. 5]." Allen calls this assertion about not being shaken or moved the "motto" of orientation.[36]

The "boundary" for the waters points up the difference between Israel and its neighbors in thinking about the world. In the ancient Near East, life was always a struggle with death, every year. In the religions of the Israelites' neighbors, the earth was a copy of heaven in which the divine personalities, each of whom personified some aspect of creation, struggled with each other in a cosmic drama. The people of these societies retold and acted out the divine drama, the primordial act of creation, to ensure order in the cosmos.

In Israelite worship, however, God is not a force in nature. Nature is God's creation and is under God's control. God has set "bounds" for it. The problem of primordial chaos is already out of the way; order does not depend on human worship each year. That God is "confident" and "serene" as Creator[37] is made clear in verse 25: The "sea" is not to be dreaded as chaos water but viewed as teeming with creatures and ships. Leviathan, the great sea monster, was created to "sport" in it.

In verses 10–13, the poet lists the different aspects of God's orderly creation; this description of nature praises God as sustainer. Springs, trees, and animals are all connected and in harmony. The center section of the psalm, verses 14–23, begins and ends with human beings at work.[38] Though the focal point of creation, they share the world; beasts of prey prowl the night, while humans work during the day. This too, is part of the order of things. Recognition of this order erupts into a mini-hymn of praise in verses 24–26.

The dependence of all of creation upon the Sustainer is made clear in verses 27–30: "All of them look to you to give them their food in due season." God did not create and withdraw but is still intimately involved in creation, which cannot exist on its own no matter how well ordered it is. When God hides the divine face or takes away their breath, "they die and return to their dust." God the Parent continually recreates.

What it means to be totally dependent upon God is amplified in the closing verses, 31–35, in which there is a return to the God of power and the theophany language of the beginning of the psalm. Just a look from this mighty Creator God and the earth "trembles"; just a touch and the mountains "smoke." There is a hint here that all is not well with God's order. The prayer in verse 35, "Let sinners be consumed from the earth, and the wicked be no more!" is addressed to God the Judge. God's careful order is challenged and disrupted by human actions, and this will not be tolerated; this is anticipated by the hiding of the divine face in verse 29. As Brueggemann puts it, "The world is a free gift from God, but with it comes an expectation and a cost. It cannot be otherwise."[39]

Psalm 104 prompts us to look around our world for signs of God's continuing creative activity. We can perhaps point most easily to the birth of babies, beautiful sunsets, and the change of seasons as signs of God the Creator at work. Yet even these are not unambiguous signs. In our technological age, we can create babies in test tubes and contribute to global warming that modifies the weather. Some even claim that creation can exist on its own without God. Psalm 104 raises an ominous challenge to our sense of self-sufficiency by asserting our ultimate dependence upon God who created us. When God hides the divine face, we are dismayed; God takes away the divine breath and we mortals die, no matter how long science can prolong our life on earth.

There are many signs today that not all is well with God's order: the homeless, drug abuse, oil spills, sexism, endangered species, inadequate schools, racism, children living below the poverty line, pollution. God the Creator is also God the Judge, who intervenes to uphold God's good intentions for creation. The look and the touch of this God can make the earth tremble and the mountains smoke. Some people do not want to see this aspect of God within Psalm 104; they claim that verses 29 and 35 "spoil" the beauty of the psalm! These verses, however, remind us that God's intentions for the created order override any of our attempts at control of the world. If we exercise a cocreatorship with God, it is because God allows us to. Verse 31b prays: "May Adonai rejoice in what Adonai makes [or has made]." We are God's creatures, part of what God makes or has made, and our activity ought to bring God joy. The expectation of Psalm 104 is that what we do on earth matters to God; this presents us with an empowering challenge.

Psalm 46: A Hymn to the God of Zion

Hymns to the God of Zion constitute a subgroup of the form-critical category of hymn; they include Psalms 46, 48, 76, 84, 87, and 122. Zion is one of the hills in Jerusalem upon which the temple was built; eventually all of Jerusalem came to be called Zion. In the hymns to the God of Zion, Zion is seen as the center, or navel, of the universe, chosen by God as the earthly center of the divine presence in the midst of the people. God's Temple and the king's palace stand on Zion.

Zion also becomes the focus for God's eschatological work for Israel and all the nations. The mythological, primeval mountain Zion will become the highest mountain to which all the nations will go up, back to the source of life, blessing, and peace. This view is expressed eloquently in Isaiah 2:1–4 and Micah 4:1–5: "It shall happen in the latter days that the mountain of the house of Adonai shall be established as the highest of the mountains . . . and peoples shall flow to it; . . . For out of Zion shall go forth the Torah, and the word of Adonai from Jerusalem [Mic. 4:1–2]."

The significance of a central, sacred place at which contact between the divine and the human worlds is made is another of the characteristics common to every people in the ancient Near East.[40] The songs of Zion in the Psalter show how Israel adapted this common cultural idea to its own unique view of God. The basic social and political unit in the ancient Near East was the city-kingdom. The city was the center of order, and the farther one moved away from it to fields and then to wilderness and desert, the more chaos threatened.

The highest point within the city, the central, sacred mountain of God, was the order core, the place within which order originated and from which it emanated to the surrounding areas. Upon this sacred mountain were situated the king's palace and the god's or goddess's temple, copies of those in heaven. Each city had its own particular god or goddess who dwelt in its temple in the city center on the sacred mountain. This god had conquered his or her chaos enemies and exercised sovereignty over all the other gods and goddesses by ordering the city and lands of the city-state. The king was the deity's ordering agent on earth.

Thus, the myth of the central, sacred place helped to explain the institutions of society and the role of the city from which dominion over a certain territory was exercised. As Joseph Campbell puts it, myth has a sociological function of "supporting and validating a certain social order"; myth is in this sense "the public dream" with which one's private dream or myth must coincide in order for one to live healthily in society.[41] When myth supports an oppressive social order, which denies the private dreams of racial groups or other minorities, then it becomes, as Brueggemann warns, a tool for social control and the status quo.

King David was the key to Israel's adaptation of this ancient Near Eastern myth of the temple city as center of the universe to support Adonai's rule in the world and Israel's hope for the future. Israel's story claimed that David had conquered Israel's Canaanite enemies and made Jerusalem his political and religious capital. By depositing in Zion the Ark of the Covenant, a kind of portable sanctuary that symbolized God's presence, David supported Israel's view of Adonai as head of the pantheon of deities, the one who defeated chaos enemies and reigned in Jerusalem. Jerusalem was the point at which contact was made between the divine and human realms, the place in which Israel's God was in control.

Some interpreters do not classify Psalm 46 as a Zion hymn, because it contains no explicit references to Zion or Jerusalem. Some do not even see it as a hymn, but rather as a psalm of confidence. Though Psalm 46 can be broken down into three sections, these sections do not correspond to the typical hymn structure of opening praise summons, motive of praise, and concluding praise summons. Psalm 46 holds together in its own way as a hymn to the God of Zion, most obviously through use of the refrain in verses 7 and 11: "Adonai of hosts is with us; the God of Jacob is our refuge." Most agree that this refrain should also conclude section one, after verse 3; some English translations do include it there. It is this idea of God as refuge, refuge in the chaotic cosmos, refuge from the hostile nations of the world, and refuge in the future of peace that ties the psalm together. The liturgical term *selah* also punctuates each section.

The first section of Psalm 46, verses 1–3, inspired Martin Luther's great Reformation hymn "A Mighty Fortress Is Our God". These verses of the psalm do not open with the customary call to praise, but rather with a declaration about God: "God is our refuge and power, a constant help in trouble."

With the language of the primordial chaos battle, verses 2 and 3 seem to describe a coming cataclysm at the end of days: "Though the earth should change, and the mountains totter into the heart of the sea." Though it is not possible for it to happen, given who

Adonai is, the mythological language here asserts that if it did, "we will not fear" because God "is a help in trouble." One can trust this God; one can feel secure in God as refuge, because God will again defeat and keep in check the chaos waters, just as God did in the primordial creation act. This language of confidence is rooted in the Genesis 1 creation story.

Section two, verses 4–7, seems to focus upon history and the nations rather than nature and the cosmos; the God of creation is the God of history. The city of God, rather than God the divine self, offers protection and refuge. Look at the transition from the roaring and foaming chaos waters of verse 3 to the "river whose streams make glad God's city" in verse 4; scene and mood change radically as we move from the first to the second section. This river recalls the river that "goes forth from Eden to water the garden, and from there is divided and becomes four rivers" in Genesis 2:10. This is a river of blessing and life, not the water of death and chaos.

Even though Zion and Jerusalem are not named, it is clear from the phrases "the city of God" and "the holy dwelling of the Most High [El Elyon]" that Psalm 46 is a Zion hymn. God's city, Jerusalem, is the place in which orderly contact is made between the great chaos water and the earth, so that the watery chaos "makes glad" the city of God, that is, serves life and order. This city, because "God is in the midst of it," "shall not totter, shall not be shaken." Here again is the motto of the oriented life. The same idea is expressed in Psalm 125:1.

Robert Alter, in his discussion of Psalm 48, applicable as well to Psalm 46, notes the paradox of the belief in one god over all the earth who yet chooses one people and one place as the medium of revelation. This paradox has a major geographical corollary; Jerusalem is the "city of our God" who is also the God of all the nations (verse 10). It is the poetry that interlocks these disparate elements and highlights the tensions.[42]

This city, Zion, is secure knowing that "God will help it by daybreak [46:5]." Even if the nations roar, Israel can trust in its God as refuge. The poet uses the same words used in verse 2 of the mountains and in verse 3 of the chaos waters, to describe the nations who attack Jerusalem in verse 6: "mountains totter, waters roar" in verses 2 and 3, and "nations roar, kingdoms totter" in verse 6. All it takes, however, is God's voice, and the nations, like waves, collapse. "God utters the divine voice; the earth melts," just as in Psalm 104:7 the waters fled at God's rebuke (compare with Psalm 29:3). This "assault of the nations" theme is a familiar one in Israelite eschatology, as for example, in Ezekiel 38, where King Gog of the land of Magog is warned of his coming defeat in his battle against God's people, Israel, so that all the nations will know Adonai. Historical events take on cosmic significance for Israel. In Psalm 46, Jerusalem, or Zion, remains secure through it all.

The eschatological picture in section three, verses 8–11, ties the first two sections together. Here the poet looks forward to the realization of God's realm on earth. Verse 8 takes a cosmic look at what happens when humans and creation oppose God—desolation. Behind this desolation is God who is working for the end of war. In verse 10 God declares, "Stop! Realize that I am God"; once the nations acknowledge God's sovereignty over the whole earth, wars will end. The Revised Standard Version translates "Be still" for the first word of verse 10, but the Hebrew means more precisely to desist, withdraw, leave off, abandon; this requires positive behavior and not simply being quiet. This is not merely war fatigue or longing for peace and rest; there is something more decisive and positive meant here. Faith in the realm of God is faith that overcomes the world and its wars and divisions.

Thus Psalm 46 moves from the story of the beginning of the world to the story of the earth's consummation in peace. That movement is supported by the reversal of imagery within the psalm. We begin with God standing still as refuge and move to the middle section, in which the city of God does not totter or shake while the waters are roaring and foaming and the nations are roaring and tottering. The psalm moves in its final section to a very active God who "breaks the bow and shatters the spear," while now it is the nations who cease activity, who are still.

Peter Craigie sees the importance of the poetry in tying the three sections of Psalm 46 together.[43] The first two sections are connected by the use of the verb *roar* in verses 3 and 6; by the use of the verb *totter or shake* in verses 2, 5, and 6; and by the noun *help* in verse 1 and the verb from the same root *will help* in verse 5. The second and third sections are tied together by the repeated use

of *nations* in verses 6 and 10 and the refrain in verses 7 and 11.
The whole psalm is woven together by the word *earth* in verses 2,
6, 8, 9, and 10; the use of this word points to God's universal
power. Unfortunately, most English translations rob us of the
poetic repetition; contemporary editors view repetition as monoto-
nous and boring and so scramble to find synonyms to substitute for
repeated words.

Psalm 46 raises for us the issue of what Walter Harrelson calls
"worship and the end."[44] Harrelson thinks it wrong to view the
eschatology of Psalm 46 or any part of the Bible as a hope in the
future that has no contact with present history. Neither is eschatology Israel's hope in the ideal spiritual condition of the
faithful in the present. "The Bible speaks of an End which moves
into the present, of a present that stretches forth toward the
consummation."[45] In worship and in faith, all of us live out of the
future and are judged by the future, by God's intention for us. Life
is not a return to a primordial time but a meeting with the future.

The picture of the End in Psalm 46 judged Israel's present and
judges the church's present today. To worship the God who puts an
end to war and brings peace is to condemn humanity's engagement
in war and racism and economic injustice. If we do not do so, God
will. You may argue that this notion seems hopelessly naive for us
today. But as Harrelson rightly insists, "There is a lure, a fascina-
tion with the image of a world set right. Believing, as we are
enabled to believe in acts of worship, that this day comes to meet
and greet us, we are propelled forward to meet the living Lord."[46]

No wonder, then, that the church associates Psalms 46 and 48
with the first Pentecost in Jerusalem (Acts 2:1–42), during which
pilgrims from all over the world were able to understand the
apostles by the power of the Holy Spirit. All the world can become
citizens of God's holy city and anticipate God's realm, even now.

What would it mean for America today if we allowed the
eschatological picture of Psalm 46 to judge our present? What
would it mean especially for our cities blighted by poverty, drugs,
violence, and despair to recover the sense of the holy city as the
contact between the divine and human realms through which
God's blessing is mediated and in which God is especially present?
It would mean a reversal of our whole attitude toward the city.
Instead of our witnessing the flight of the church from the city to

the suburbs, we would see churches witnessing in the inner city to the God who intends blessing for us all. Order would once again flow from the city center to the surrounding areas instead of in the reverse direction as it does now. We would perhaps discover that it is not "us" against "them," especially "those" blacks and Latinos and Asians, but that we are all "refugees" seeking the "refuge" of the God of Jacob; all of humanity is a "refugee."[47] In that discovery there awaits our humanity and wholeness and God's realm.

Chapter 3

You Get What You Deserve, Don't You?

The Torah and Wisdom Psalms

The psalms called wisdom psalms and Torah psalms, like the hymn psalms we considered in chapter 2, also articulate the season of orientation, of well-orderedness. Unlike the hymn psalms, they do not constitute a recognizable literary type or form, but rather distinguish themselves by their content and world view. Psalms 1, 19, and 119 are all classified as Torah psalms. The Septuagint (Greek translation of Hebrew Scripture) translates *Torah* as "law," but the word means much more than that. Torah means God's "instruction" or "guidance" for Israel, which includes law but also poetry, story, saga, and genealogy. Jews call the first five books of Hebrew Scripture the Torah.

In Israel, Torah and creation are understood together, for Torah is the way by which Israel responds to God's well-ordered creation. As Brueggemann argues, "The good order of creation is concretely experienced in Israel as the *torah*."[1] Psalm 19 makes this connection explicit. The first six verses are a hymn to God the Creator: God's handiwork, the heavens, "tell the glory of God," while verses 7–14 meditate upon the Torah of Adonai.[2] The heavens may reveal God in general, but Torah reveals Adonai, the One who redeemed Israel from slavery and entered into covenant. The sun may give light and heat (verse 6), but Torah is "radiant" and "enlightens the eyes" (verse 8). The praise of God in creation and

43

in Torah leads to an awareness of the psalmist's own place in creation and relation to God, which issues in a prayer for forgiveness: "Clear me from hidden faults [v. 12]." In this sense, Psalm 19 could be called a psalm of new orientation, for embracing Torah prompts self-examination and a critique of the status quo.

Verses 10 and 11 declare that the ordinances of Adonai's Torah are sweeter than honey and "in keeping them there is great reward." Psalm 19 defines the reward that results from keeping Torah in terms of the simple being made wise, the heart rejoicing, and the eyes being enlightened, rather than in terms of material aggrandizement. This is what happens when one lives in harmony with God's intentions. That there is reward in keeping Torah links Psalm 19 to wisdom psalms, which also lift up the idea of certain actions having certain consequences.

In Hebrew, the word for wisdom is *hokmah;* the Greek equivalent is *sophia,* both feminine terms. In Hebrew Scripture, wisdom means many things: skill, as in the artistic or technical skill of the farmer, the sailor, the artisan, the diplomat, and the king; cleverness or cunning, in terms of being able to seize the moment and make the best of every situation; the art of living, in terms of behavior and attitudes toward life; religion or faith, for "the fear of Adonai is the beginning of wisdom [Prov. 9:10; Job 28:28; Ps. 111:10]."

In Proverbs 1, 8, and 9, wisdom is personified as Woman Wisdom who is preacher, friend, hostess, lover. (There are some similarities between Woman Wisdom and the woman of worth of Proverbs 31.) Ultimately, however, wisdom cannot be defined; it is hidden. As Job 28:12 asks, "But where can wisdom be found?" "It is hidden from the eyes of all living [v. 21]"; "God understands the way to it and knows its place [v. 23]." In this sense, wisdom is the principle that holds the world together, the order given by God to the world. God alone has access to it; it is beyond human limitations.

In Hebrew Scripture, the books of Proverbs, Job, Qoheleth (Ecclesiastes), and some psalms are considered to be wisdom literature. Sirach (Ecclesiasticus) and the Wisdom of Solomon, in the Apocrypha or Deuterocanon, are also wisdom works. Other cultures in the ancient Near East, especially Mesopotamia and Egypt, produced an extensive wisdom literature. Wisdom thinking was not unique to Israel but an international movement.

Wisdom literature articulates a particular world view, or way of looking at things.[3] Wisdom is (1) anthropocentric. This means that it is centered on human beings rather than on God. Wisdom asks, "What is good for us?"

Wisdom is (2) pragmatic. Thought and behavior are evaluated according to whether or not they yield practical, life-enhancing results. What enhances life is good; what detracts from life is bad.

Wisdom is also (3) experiential. Wisdom is a human search; it does not talk about the will of God. The answers to life's questions can be learned from experience and discovered by human reason; the parable is undergirded by this understanding. The sage, or wise person who teaches wisdom, makes no claim to divine authority. The validity of the sage's teaching stands or falls on whether or not human experience confirms it.

Wisdom is (4) universal. Wisdom is open to all; it can be discovered by human intelligence. Wisdom is not the property of an elite but assumes a oneness and order from God about the world. A search for wisdom is a search for order and the effort to live in harmony with that order. Wisdom in its universal sense can lead the church away from narrow concerns of denomination to broader human problems.

Wisdom is (5) optimistic. Successful living is within everyone's grasp: just follow the sage's advice. A modern distortion of the optimism of wisdom can be seen in "the power of positive thinking" and "success through prayer"; if you do not succeed, it's all your fault—you just haven't prayed or thought hard enough.

In order to articulate this way of looking at things through wisdom, the sage used riddles, debate, didactic narratives, and the proverb, or *mashal,* a short, pithy saying that sums up some observed truth or fact of human experience, as for example, Proverbs 12:19: "Truthful lips endure forever, but a lying tongue is but for a moment [RSV]." Wisdom themes range from concern about table manners, laziness, proper speech, drunkenness, and anger, to God's justice and the inescapability of death. Think for a minute about modern proverbs, many of which have found their way onto bumper stickers. Today we, too, try to sum up life and make sense of it.

One of the most prominent themes in wisdom thought is the theme of "two ways": the way of the wicked leads to punishment and death; the way of the righteous, to reward and life. The wise choose the righteous way, for its natural outcome is blessing; only a fool would choose the wicked way, for it leads naturally and inevitably to disaster. This theme of the two ways is also called divine retribution, act/consequence, or "you get what you deserve." Proverbs 11:21 states it succinctly: "Be assured, an evil person will not go unpunished, but the children of the righteous will be safe."[4]

We don't think about this idea all the time in the ordinary run of things, especially when things are going well for us. However, as soon as something goes wrong and we are confronted by a tragedy, it is very likely that our first thoughts will be "Why me?" "What did I do to deserve this?" Though questioning of this type is clearly expressed by the wisdom literature, it permeates the entire Bible and even our liturgies.

For example, in Deuteronomy, we find Moses in 30:15–20 exhorting the Israelites to choose the right way: "I have set before you life and death, blessing and curse; therefore choose life, that you and your descendants may live [v. 19 RSV]." One chooses life by keeping covenant, by obeying the commandments. The choice rests with us, and we must suffer the consequences of choosing wrongly.

The Israelite prophets offer their prophecies of disaster based upon the same principle of act/consequence. In Amos 6:4–7, for example, Amos warns: "Woe to those who lie upon beds of ivory . . . but are not grieved over the ruin of Joseph! Therefore they shall now be the first of those to go into exile [RSV]." Similar passages are found in Isaiah 3:16–17 and 5:8–10; Jeremiah 6:8–12 and 14:10; and Micah 2:1–5. The prophets connect the disobedience of the people with their coming punishment. In the same way, Deutero Isaiah preaches "comfort, comfort" to the people Israel in exile, for they have received from Adonai's hand double for all their sins.

The whole Deuteronomistic History (Joshua, Judges, 1 and 2 Samuel, and 1 and 2 Kings), which was probably brought together and edited in exile, views Israel's entire history as an articulation of "you get what you deserve." The cycle of apostasy, punishment, repentance, and forgiveness, which is so clear in Judges (for example, 3:7–12) and the rest of the books in this grouping, gives hope to the exiles. History is not over, for if they repent, God will deliver them.

In the New Testament, Galatians 6:7–10 declares: "Do not be deceived; God is not mocked, for whatever one sows, that one will also reap." In Matthew 7:13–14, many enter the wide gate to destruction, while few enter the narrow gate to life. This is a theme similar to that in the story of the wise and foolish virgins in Matthew 25:1–13. In Romans 1:18, God's wrath is revealed against the ungodly and wicked. Paul asserts in Romans 8:6 that "to set the mind on the flesh is death, but to set the mind on the Spirit is life and peace [RSV]." Act/consequence permeates the Letter of James. The Beatitudes (Matthew 5:1–12) affirm that the meek, the merciful, the mourners all deserve God's blessing, an affirmation of "you get what you deserve" that reverses society's judgments about who is blessed. In our liturgies we assume that repentance, in the form of our confession of sin, will bring God's forgiveness. It is only after that forgiveness that we dare to offer petitionary prayers.

There are many ways in which we affirm the theory of act/consequence in our daily lives. The American legal system upholds act/consequence: If you break the law, you are punished. Debate centers on whether or not the punishment "fits" the crime; that is, did this person get what she or he deserved? We evaluate illness and tragedy, success and wealth according to the reward/punishment idea: "How could Mrs. Brown get cancer? She's such a nice person, always helping everybody; it's not fair"; "Why should Mr. White drive such a fancy car and get such a long vacation? He's so mean at work, a real back-stabber; he doesn't deserve it"; "Why should Ann get better grades than I do when I work so hard and she never studies?" Often we seek at least a balancing out of the good and the bad in our lives. How many times have you heard someone say, "My kids have been sick on and off for a year with ear infections and strep throat, the roof leaks, my husband didn't get his raise—everything seems to come at once. I'm due for a good year now." Psalm 90 expresses the same idea in a petition to God in verse 15: "Make us glad as many days as you have made us miserable, as many years as we have seen misfortune."

The problem with the theory of act/consequence is that it can very easily become a way in which we victimize the victim. Working backward from the consequence, that is, from sickness or material success or whatever, we place more emphasis upon the result than upon the act itself and what caused it. This is what Job's friends did; they saw Job sick on the dung heap, bereft of family and wealth, and they automatically assumed that he had done something wrong to "deserve" that kind of "punishment." Because their minds were made up about it, they could not listen sympathetically to Job's protestations; and, more important, they did not hear Job's pain. They acted like district attorneys rather than like friends and comforters and were thus unable to do anything to affect the act or the consequence. Churches that do not hold God's grace in tension with God's judgment but over-emphasize the harsh nature of a God who calls us to account, reinforce the belief that we get what we deserve in this negative way.

This distorted, backward application of "you get what you deserve" has alarming social implications. There are some in America who view the statistics on the number of blacks and Latinos in jail as a confirmation of the inferiority of races. They "deserve" to be in jail, because they are lazy or unintelligent or evil. The social conditions of poverty and substandard education, which contribute to minority crime, are dismissed. On the other hand, those in control, who are successful, attribute their success to their own goodness and superiority. If "those" people cannot "make it" as we did, then it's their fault. Not only do we see this in relation to American society, but also on a global scale. The United States basks in its world power and pats itself on the back for its industriousness and virtue. If countries in the Third World are poor, it's their fault. If we could make a success of ourselves, so can they; they're just not trying hard enough. The result of such self-righteousness is social control and injustice.

How might our affirmation of act/consequence serve to critique and transform our society and promote justice instead of contribute to the status quo and social control? We could focus on the action and what causes it, rather than on the consequence, so that new behavior can have positive, life-enhancing consequences. Many churches have begun to lobby for affordable housing in their communities, to provide decent day-care programs for working mothers, especially those in one-parent households, to operate homeless shelters and soup kitchens, and to educate against drug abuse. This approach to act/consequence can empower rather than doom people. It takes seriously the dignity of every person and our responsibility to one another, as well as God's good intention for us all. When act/consequence becomes a private yardstick for an individual or a specific nation, it can become a whipping stick rather than a shepherd's crook to draw us closer together as the people of God. Act/consequence can be a way for us all to live in the way God intends. The charge that Moses in Deuteronomy 30:19 put to the Israelites as they were about to enter into the promised land of Canaan is one that we also must heed today: "Life and death I have set before you, blessing and curse; choose life, that you and your descendants may live [RSV]."

Psalm 1: Gateway to the Psalter

Psalm 1 can be called both a Torah psalm and a wisdom psalm. It is a wisdom psalm in that the theme of the two ways is clearly articulated by the contrast between the righteous and the wicked. Also, act/consequence is encapsulated in the proverb upon which the psalm is built in verse 6: "For Adonai knows the way of the righteous, but the way of the wicked will perish." It is a Torah psalm in that delighting in and meditating upon the Torah of Adonai marks the way of the righteous person.

It is fruitful to think about why the editor of the Psalter recognized the appropriateness of placing Psalm 1 at the head of the collection. The context for praying, singing, or preaching the rest of the psalms is set by Psalm 1 and its declaration of the two ways and the joy of Torah. Psalm 1 serves, in effect, as our guidepost at the entrance to the Psalter; it helps us to keep our bearings through our life's journey, because it tells us that Torah articulates God's intention for us. As Brueggemann argues, Psalm 1 "announces that the primary agenda for Israel's worship life is obedience"; how we choose to live our life matters in terms of God's purpose for creation. Furthermore, the beginning and end of the Psalter, Psalms 1 and 150, are connected in that "a life grounded in obedience leads precisely to doxology."[5]

The first half of the proverb in verse 6 of Psalm 1 concerning the righteous is taken up in the opening verses 1–3. The righteous are defined negatively, which also introduces their contrast with the wicked. The righteous are those who do not walk, stand, or sit with sinners; in short, they have nothing to do with those whose way is wicked, for the three verbs encompass all human activity.

The righteous are "blessed" ('ashre, literally "happy, fortunate") which, as Fred Craddock argues, means "favored of God"; pronouncing them so actually conveys blessing.[6] Just as the Beatitudes at the beginning of the Sermon on the Mount bless, or announce God's favor, before instructions are given or obedience required, so the righteous are pronounced blessed before they make their way through the Psalter. God's blessing is the context for our journey of faith. Are we able to accept this blessing? As Craddock observes, "It is more difficult to hear and receive a blessing than to attempt to achieve one."[7]

This perhaps explains why so many people are uncomfortable with the either/or contrast between righteous and wicked in Psalm 1. Most of us would like to see a bit more ambiguity than the psalm allows, for we don't seem completely to be either one or the other, either wicked or righteous. The real problem is that we cannot accept the blessing God holds out to us up front as pure grace. That became clear to me when I visited a terminal cancer patient in the hospital. I was surprised by the fact that Psalm 1 was her favorite psalm; "God knows I am trying to be righteous, and that's enough," she said. What a humble acceptance of God's blessing! From all the psalms that follow Psalm 1 in the Psalter, we know and God knows how difficult the life of faith is, yet we are blessed as we begin our faith journey.

Negatively, the righteous one avoids the wicked; positively, she or he delights in and meditates upon Adonai's Torah, and in that activity discovers the meaning of life. The righteous one is "like a tree planted by streams of water," deeply rooted and nourished. Just as a tree planted by a stream would flourish because of its constant water supply, so a person rooted in Torah would "prosper" because of her or his constant instruction from God.

Prosper is an unfortunate word choice of the Revised Standard Version translation; many people think immediately of material success and wealth. The righteous have the Midas touch! But that is not what is meant here. The New Jewish Version of the Jewish Publication Society translates more appropriately "thrive." To "thrive" is to live within guidelines set by God, to be "known" (verse 6) by God in the sense of "embraced" (Alter, *The Art of Biblical Poetry*), "looked after," "cherished." This means that one is whole and in relationship with God, even when in the pit of disorientation, even when and especially when one is troubled.

To be prosperous and to delight in Torah does not mean that

one is sheltered from the problems of the world; the guidance of Torah helps one through problems. The tree planted by the stream is not necessarily protected from strong winds, flood, or drought; neither does it yield fruit all the time or any time it wants to, but "in its season," that is, at the proper time. As one parishioner on the Eastern Shore of Maryland told his pastor, "I'm prosperous." This was an old man who had been a fisherman all his life, who was not rich at all and, in fact, just made enough to get by. But he was weathered and solid; he'd been through it all and prevailed, just like the deeply rooted tree by the stream. I think Craigie is right when he argues that blessedness is not a reward but rather the natural result of a particular type of life.[8] Torah is the way one should naturally go; that way is not a burden but a delight.

The antithetical idea of righteous/wicked is sharpened in verse 4: "Not so the wicked." This abrupt declaration denies any rootedness to the wicked at all; they do not thrive. Instead, they are "like chaff which the wind drives away." They are winnowed out of the "congregation of the righteous [v. 5]"; they are too unstable, worthless, and light to "stand in the judgment." The wicked just can't compare with the kernel of grain that is too heavy for the wind to blow away; the wicked cannot endure. This point is emphasized by the fact that it takes only three lines of poetry to dismiss the wicked but six lines of poetry to plant the righteous.

The poetic language of Psalm 1 actually makes the idea of act/consequence seem built into the very structure of reality. As Alter[9] points out, indicators clue us in to the transition between righteous and wicked at the beginning of verse 2 ("but, or rather"), verse 4 ("not so"), verse 5 ("thus, or therefore"), and verse 6 ("for"). The verbs in the poem depict the wicked in constant motion, restless, without direction, carried away as objects by forces over which they have no control. The righteous, however, are "planted," a passive participle, as they meditate. The envelope structure of the psalm, in which the end formally echoes the beginning, also anchors this idea that you get what you deserve. The psalm begins and ends with the wicked, resha'im. Into their midst, but not associating with them, come the righteous. The way of sinners, which the righteous avoid (verse 1), leads nowhere; it perishes (verse 6).

Psalm 1 makes it clear that how we choose to live our lives

matters to God. When we choose the right path and obey God, God embraces us and we thrive. This is not to say that we will never experience hardship or pain, but if we do, God is with us and cares for us. Psalm 1 shows us a God who is a powerful judge ("the way of the wicked will perish") but also a loyal caregiver who blesses us on our journey through life. This psalm holds up Torah, God's instruction, as a standard against which we can judge our behavior toward one another. There is a right way to live life, and it does matter, not only to God, but to those with whom we live in community. Do we walk, stand, or sit with those who trivialize God by straying from the right path God has set out for us? If we do, then our community is harmed. We don't want to make trouble or get involved, so we look the other way when someone does something wrong and excuse it by arguing that "it was a little infraction" or "it won't really hurt anyone." Do we let our standards of human conduct slide when it's to our advantage or when it's just the easier thing to do? In a world in which it seems that "anything goes," Psalm 1 calls us back to God as our center and standard and to faithful conduct toward one another.

Psalm 37: Success of the Wicked?

Psalm 37 is also a wisdom psalm but does not declare so boldly that "you get what you deserve." Rather, it appends a qualifier: "Don't you?" This is clear from verse 1: "Do not fret because of the wicked; do not be envious of wrongdoers." Obviously, the wicked are not getting what they deserve; they are doing well enough to be envied. This psalm struggles with the painful picture of the wicked prospering while the righteous suffer.

Many have dismissed this as a forced struggle, because the psalm unfolds in the form of an acrostic; the first letter of every verse or every other verse is a successive letter of the Hebrew alphabet. This acrostic form is, of course, impossible to detect in English translations. Psalm 37 is dismissed as a mere hodge-podge of proverbs strung together in this artificial way. But Brueggemann reminds us about the pedagogical purpose of an acrostic: "The carefully ordered arrangement corresponds to the claim made for the substance of the psalm; that is, the world is exceedingly well

ordered, and virtue is indeed rewarded."[10] The theme of act/
consequence permeates the psalm and ties it together.

In order to deal with the apparent breakdown in the wisdom
claim that you get what you deserve, the sage gives advice to those
who are fretting. In keeping with the wisdom world view, the sage's
advice is practical, experiential, and human-centered. See how
many pieces of advice you can identify within Psalm 37. You have
probably given similar advice to your friends or to your children
many times.

Psalm 37 begins with advice: "Do not fret" (also verse 7). Why?
"For like the grass they soon wither" (verse 2; compare with verse
20); the apparent success of the wicked is temporary. Verse 10,
"Yet a little while and the wicked will be no more [RSV]," repeats
this observation. All you need to do is "wait patiently" (verse 7
and also verse 34), and things will work out as they should. While
you wait for the wicked to vanish, "trust in Adonai" (verse 3 and
again in verse 5) and "delight in Adonai" (verse 4).

To trust means that you must "commit your way to Adonai"
(verse 5), "be patient" (verse 7), and "refrain from anger" (verse 8).
Wisdom thinking holds up control and silence as proper behavior
that leads to successful living; passion and an unbridled tongue
mark the way of the fool. In a similar way, our patriarchal society
today values "the poker face" and the "stiff upper lip" as marks of
control and authority. Against this standard women are often seen
as too emotional and therefore weak and not worthy of trust. (Yet,
compare this minimizing of women's abilities and capacities to the
very positive view of Woman Wisdom in Proverbs 1–9 and of the
woman of worth in Proverbs 31.)

Why fret when even Adonai "laughs at the wicked" because
"their day is coming" (Psalm 37:13)? The wicked will not be able
to escape the consequences of their actions. The sage shares some
proverbs in verses 16, 18, and 21 to undergird the advice given.
The sage counsels not only refraining from certain behavior and
thoughts but also acting positively in order to deal with the
situation: "Turn from evil and do good" (verse 27; also verse 3).
One cannot just sit back and let God do it all; one needs vision
and purposeful activity to live through and beyond the present
painful situation. One must keep to God's way (verses 5, 23, 34),
and that requires very positive action.

What personal testimony does the sage offer up to support the advice given? "I have been young and now have grown old; yet I have not seen the righteous forsaken or their children begging bread" (verse 25). How many times have you heard from someone older than you, your parents or grandparents, that they've lived longer and can tell you a thing or two! A second time the sage insists: "I have seen the wicked powerful and spreading like a native green tree; again I passed by, and they were no more" (verses 35–36). What is your reaction to this testimony?

Your first response is probably, Where has this person been? Is this a hermit who's been hiding in a cave? Just open the newspaper and turn on the TV and see how these statements are contradicted! Walk down the street and see the homeless, the addicted, the abused. At first glance these testimonies of the sage seem grossly out of step with reality. Our experience just doesn't confirm them. Besides, nowadays old age just does not guarantee that one is more experienced than someone else; children grow up fast. On one level, then, Psalm 37 underscores the dangers of an unreflected faith, of closing one's eyes to the reality of the world and its brokenness. Psalm 37 can be used in this way for social control and the perpetuation of injustice.

On another level, however, Psalm 37 can be used very positively for social critique and transformation. It speaks of God's purposes for our life, for behavior that is in harmony with God's intention for order. The sage asserts that "God loves justice" (verse 28), and the psalm seems to say that this justice involves our doing good (verses 3 and 27), being generous and giving (verse 21), giving liberally and lending (verse 26), and uttering wisdom and speaking justice (verse 30). We must ask ourselves if we are doing that; only then may we be counted among the righteous.

The sage does not ignore the fact that God's justice is not evidenced in the world. The sage acknowledges that "the wicked plots against the righteous [v. 12, RSV]," that "the wicked watches the righteous seeking to kill them [v. 32]," and that "the wicked draw the sword . . . to bring down the poor and the needy [v. 14, RSV]." The life of faith is not easy; if it were, then the sage would not have to repeat so often the advice to have patience, wait for God, trust.

The kind of faith that motivates the psalmist accepts and

endures the tensions of this life, tensions between what cannot be seen and yet what must be believed. The psalmist believes that "the meek shall inherit the land and enjoy themselves with great well-being [v. 11]"; Jesus in the Sermon on the Mount knew this type of faith (Matthew 5:5). Psalm 37's insistence upon the meek inheriting in the face of the wicked raises the issue of how long an oppressed people can wait for that to happen and what to do in the meantime. In the face of the continued suffering of the black community, womanist (black feminist) theologians are beginning to fashion a new paradigm of redemptive suffering; black suffering has meaning and redemptive power because it confronts institutional evils such as racism and sexism. Only the oppressed can develop this paradigm, however. The oppressors have no right, for redemptive suffering too quickly can become a support for oppression—"suffering is good for you."

Psalm 37 makes it clear that it is more important to behave in positive ways than it is to worry about those who are doing well and not getting what they deserve. This psalm makes it difficult to blame somebody else for our problems and pushes us to take responsibility for our own part in the world. Psalm 37 does not claim that life is easy and that the sage's advice is easily followed. Rather, it observes that energy wasted in envy could better be spent doing good, being generous, lending and speaking justly. We must ask ourselves whether this observation can be applied to our lives today, whether at work or at home. Do we spend more time complaining about a colleague at work than doing better at our own job? Do we compare our children to other children and wonder why ours don't do as well at school or at sports, when, rather than waste time comparing, we could be spending more time with them playing ball or going over homework or just talking? Do we lament the crime and drug abuse in our neighborhoods but fail to volunteer our time and energy to get at their root causes?

All of the wisdom psalms point beyond ourselves to a reality that endures and gives us direction: God. Wisdom psalms focus upon our behavior as central to God's blessing: "Adonai embraces the way of the righteous, but the way of the wicked will perish." How we define who the righteous and the wicked are in the wisdom psalms says a great deal about how we apply these psalms to our own life. It is dangerous to claim that the righteous are only those who are just like us, that is, with the same color skin or comparable income, or that the wicked are those who are "different." If wisdom is truly universal and not the possession of an elite, then there are practical, life-enhancing things we can do, not only for ourselves and those like us, but also for others not like us. This is the way of wisdom; this is justice, and "Adonai loves justice" (Psalm 37:28). Do we?

Chapter 4

Complaining in Faith to God

Psalm Laments

Nearly one-third of the 150 psalms in the Psalter are laments, which articulate the experience of disorientation in the life of an individual or in the corporate life of Israel. Most of the laments are the so-called angry, or imprecatory, laments, which find the present situation of distress unfair and inexplicable and complain about it to God. Only the seven penitential laments (Psalms 6, 32, 38, 51, 102, 130, and 143) accept the experience of suffering as deserved punishment for sin. Among the corporate (in contrast to the individual) laments, those that mention the people's sin do not see the people's suffering as just punishment but as excessive and thus undeserved.

Despite the fact that laments are so numerous, they are seldom used in Christian worship. People are often surprised to find laments in the Bible at all, considering them to be "unchristian." Occasionally we find an angry lament as a responsive reading in the back of our hymnals but with all of the angry parts cut out. At best, the church uses the seven penitential laments during the lenten season, for these psalms articulate lenten penitential themes. Psalm 51, for example, poignantly pleads: "Grace me, O God, according to your *ḥesed,* according to your abundant womb-love, blot out my transgressions. Wash me thoroughly from my iniquity and cleanse me from my sin."

There are times in our lives when our acknowledgment of sin rightly moves us to confession and petition for God's forgiveness; but there are other times when we honestly do not understand why we suffer, and we question angrily rather than confess. In light of these other times, we must ask with Roland Murphy whether "we have lost the art of complaining *in faith* to God in favor of a stoic concept of what obedience or resignation to the divine will really means."[1]

Many Christians think that "complaining in faith" is a contradiction in terms; if one complains, one is not faithful. This view comes to the fore in a comment I heard recently from a pastor: "I deal with a lot of widows trying to cope with the change in their situation. Of course once they've asked the question 'why me?' they've already lost their faith, so a lot of rebuilding has to be done."

This seems to be a harsh comment, doesn't it? Have you ever said anything like that? Your response is probably no, but think about how this view emerges in other things that we say and do when someone is hurting. When my twenty-three-year-old brother drowned, many well-meaning people came to the funeral home and said to my sobbing mother, "Have faith, Rose." Their comments suggested that her sobs and anger and questions of why were unfaithful responses to the pain of her loss. She certainly took the comments that way, which added more anger and also guilt to her pain.

The question "why me?" (or "why my brother?") is undergirded by the theory of act/consequence discussed in chapter 3. "Why me?" means "what did I do to deserve this?" Parents who have lost a child in an accident or to a disease like cancer will review their efforts on the child's behalf and wonder, "What good does any of it do? We've done all the right things all our lives; everything was planned out carefully. We thought that if we lived the way we should, things would work out the way we wanted. It just doesn't seem fair." In their assessment, they and their child did not get what was deserved.

The failure of act/consequence in our experience of death or prolonged illness is exacerbated by cultural values and assumptions about health. We operate under the illusion that we can control our lives if we exercise, eat right, wear the right clothes, and manage our stress. We expect to stay young and avoid death if we do all these things. Think of all the TV and newspaper advertisements for instant pain relief, health spas, and food, which drive home this theme. When a child dies, however, or an elderly parent succumbs after a long and painful illness, our sense is that things are no longer under our control. Life is not supposed to be this way if we play by all the rules. The ordering of our lives according to the idea that we get what we deserve is challenged by our experience of inexplicable disorientation.

Cultural values about health are just a slice of what Brueggemann calls the dominant American cultural ideology of success, continuity, and the avoidance of anything messy like pain and loss in all areas of our life. Again, TV and radio advertisements that would have us believe the right bank or life insurance policy is the key to success, sitcoms that resolve gut-wrenching problems in thirty minutes, and the difficulty of attracting and holding people in the caring professions—all are symptomatic of our cultural unwillingness to deal with the painful reality of our human situation.

Despite the illusion of our success, we experience repeated challenges to the order and reliability of life, which shake our confidence in the One who keeps order. These challenges move us out of orientation into disorientation. In our move, which the laments enable us to articulate in a way that matches our experience, "we engage in a countercultural activity,"[2] because our disorientating experiences fly in the face of the dominant cultural ideology of success.

There are many different kinds of losses, besides the death or illness of a loved one, that can push us into disorientation and challenge our cultural illusions. Divorce, loss of a job, a partner's adultery, substance abuse by a member of one's family, AIDS, chronic illness, child abuse, spouse abuse, rape—all confront our individual perceptions of orientation, security of a well-ordered world, and the notion that we are in control or that God oversees the running of a well-ordered world. We also experience communal losses and disorientation: Toxic waste dumps threaten the health of whole communities; racism in our schools and work places divides blacks, whites, Latinos, and Asian Americans; national trade deficits and international terrorism threaten our national pride and place in the world.

Whatever our experience of loss, our movement out of orientation into the pit of disorientation is one that society does not acknowledge or support. This lack of support is evidenced in many ways, because society evaluates different pits of disorientation differently. Even minimal support levels vary depending upon whether a personal loss is from accidental death, divorce, mental illness, substance addiction, or AIDS. Societal evaluation of communal losses is even more complex; communities are fragmented and diverse today, and we are not often willing to become involved unless we are directly affected.

When my brother died, my father as a blue-collar worker was allowed only three days off from work for his grief process. Yet even though this timetable seemed insensitive, his coworkers almost tiptoed around him deferentially; his son was a good boy, Phi Beta Kappa, top 10 percent of his class at the University of Michigan Law School, not a drug addict or homosexual with AIDS. If that had not been the case, would his coworkers have kept their awkward, respectful silence; or would they have said something purposefully hurtful, implying that he got what he deserved?

How can we deal with disorientation if our culture will not acknowledge our questions as we make the painful move into disorientation? Will the church listen? The fact that the angry laments have been so little used in our liturgies suggests not. Our pastor may meet with us to help us work through the pain, but without the larger support of the community of faith that is the church, this isolated care will be helpful but incomplete. Does the community of mutual caring that is the church care enough about the pain of its members to make room for the lament in its liturgical life, teaching, and counseling?

Lament language can help the church speak the truth about human experience and the life of faith. By ignoring or suppressing the laments, the church turns its back on a canonical witness to the struggle for faith in God. Why does the church cut itself off from a valuable resource for healing and wholeness within the brokenness and suffering of our world?

A form-critical analysis of the lament structure can help to show why the lament can be called a legitimate complaint in faith to God and how the lament can contribute to our healing and wholeness. I will illustrate the parts of the lament structure with verses taken from different laments, then treat selected individual and communal laments in their entirety. The structure outlined below is an ideal structure only; not every lament will correspond to this form in every detail. In fact, it is the deviation from the conventional, the move away from the norm, that often contributes to the meaning of a psalm. One can identify all the parts of a lament, but the investigation of a lament psalm should be a new way of seeing both the psalm and ourselves whole. In this way, lamenting can be a healing process. (Outline items 1, 2, 3 and 4 appear in this chapter; 5 and 6, in chapter 5.)

The Structure of the Lament

1. Address
   a. Short, emotion-packed
   b. Why? How long?
2. Complaint proper
   a. The psalmist's suffering (I/we)
   b. The enemies (they)
   c. God accused of not caring/doing (You)
3. Petition
4. Motivations
   a. Confession of sin
   b. Protestation of innocence
   c. Public relations value of psalmist
5. Confession of trust
   a. Usually introduced by *but*
   b. Faith that knows what it is talking about
6. Vow of praise

As can be seen from its structure, a lament does not merely bemoan hardship but rather seeks change. It means to get something from God and thus "is primarily an appeal."[3] A lament psalm describes a distress, interprets it, and appeals to God based on that interpretation. The psalmist's intention is to motivate God's intervention. In order to motivate, lament langauge is vivid and metaphorical, evocative and provocative. It seeks God's involvement to change the situation of distress. Lament language is intense, because it is language at the extremities of life, language in the pit of disorientation.

If we are to enter the world of the lament, we need to enter into the intensity and emotion of lament poetry, rather than judge it or be shocked by it. How ironic that there is very little that seems to shock us in the secular world anymore. Hollywood stars and "ordinary" people share the most intimate details of their lives with millions of people on the TV and radio talk shows. Just let people say exactly what's on their mind to God in prayer, however, and shock and pious censure are our immediate response! What a wedge we drive between the secular and sacred in our lives! How can we possibly be whole before God when we split our lives in two this way?

Address

The lament address is usually very short and packed with emotion, as for example, in Psalm 22:1: "My God, my God, why have you forsaken me?" In Matthew 27:46 (compare with Mark 15:34), Jesus takes up these words as his last on the cross. Jesus' lament on the cross signals that Lent can be a way into our pain and that of the world, a way to acknowledge and articulate that pain, a way that may not always begin with repentance but sometimes with questions and doubts.

The address is actually a minifaith statement, clearly identifying the One to whom the psalmist prays. The address suggests that this One matters to the psalmist; if not, why would she or he bother to pray to God in the first place? By naming God, the psalmist asserts that God is the source of healing, the One who can overcome the present distress.

The use of the possessive adjective *my* in the address of Psalm 22 claims an intimate past relationship with God, which underscores the present distress and undergirds the later petition for intervention. The psalmist, in effect, reminds God of their relationship and the expectations surrounding that relationship. This verse also shows how often an exclamation or a rhetorical question is interwoven with the identification of God in the lament. These questions actually belong to the complaint proper.

The Hebrew question *lamah* (why) is the most frequently occurring question in the psalms. It is not simply a question of information, as if God could explain the pain away. The why indicates that something is very wrong and that the psalmist does not understand what is happening and feels totally helpless; otherwise the following petitions for God to intervene would not make any sense.

As Harold Kushner points out about Job's friends, their first mistake was to think that when Job asked "Why is God doing this to me?" he was asking a question that they could answer and that their answer would be helpful. "In reality, Job's words were not a theological question at all, but a cry of pain,"[4] requiring an exclamation point rather than a question mark. Job's friends were so busy doing theology (talking about God) that they almost forgot about Job; they did not show any sympathy to the one on the dung heap. Their pastoral sensitivity was strongest when they sat with Job in silence for seven days and seven nights!

Whereas the why question in laments is full of reproach and accusation of God, the also frequent "how long?" expresses the urgency of the painful situation. Both are rhetorical questions. "How long?" is also not a question for information, as if knowing that the pain would end in six weeks or three months or one year would satisfy the psalmist and make everything all right. Rather, the psalmist asks "how long?" to assert, "This has gone on long enough![5] I can't take it any more!"

Complaint Proper

The largest part of the lament psalm is usually the description of the distress, a setting forth of what is wrong. Language in this section is highly metaphorical and figurative. It is meant to be provocative and evocative, to draw us into sympathy and outrage.

Both God and the community of faith that hears the psalm must be convinced of the intensity of the suffering and the need for God to act. The complaint may contain one, two, or three foci: (1) the one lamenting and her or his suffering, or the community's suffering (I/we); (2) the enemies (they); and (3) God, who is accused of not caring or not doing or of acting in the wrong way (You).

The Psalmist's Suffering (I/We)

One cannot remain unmoved by the very emotional language describing the sufferer's distress. The psalmist in Psalm 22:14–15, for example, cries out: "I am poured out like water, and all my bones are out of joint; my heart is like wax, it is melted within my breast; my strength is dried up like a potsherd, and my tongue cleaves to my jaws; thou dost lay me in the dust of death [RSV; a potsherd is a piece of a broken pottery jug or jar]." Bracketing out for now the fact that Jesus, according to the Gospels of Matthew and Mark, used the first verse of Psalm 22 from the cross and that these words of suffering can be applied to him, what do you think the psalmist is suffering from? What is wrong?

To be "poured out like water" suggests fatigue and exhaustion, either physical or spiritual. People with arthritis have pointed to the "bones out of joint" as an indication of their condition. The "tongue cleaving to the jaws" always reminds me of the cancer patients I visited in the hospital who had just come back from their chemotherapy treatments and could not drink anything. All they could do was suck on an ice cube to reduce the terrible dryness in their mouths. Note how the I/we of the complaint moves into the You of complaint, to God, in the last part of verse 15. God is seen as the source of the psalmist's pain. The psalmist's suffering is the result of God's action: "*You* lay me in the dust of death" (italics added).

Though scholars have tried to uncover the specific circumstances that evoked this description of suffering, most agree that to do so is impossible. If five people were asked to write down what they thought the psalmist's distress was in Psalm 22, they would probably give five different answers. This illustrates the beauty and staying power of stylized psalm language, which describes in a vivid way shared situations of suffering. Thus, the same psalm can be

used by different people in varied circumstances. Today we can
plug into psalm descriptions of suffering at many different points in
our lives and particularize them with our own personal experience.
The image of suffering suggested to us today in Psalm 22:14–15
may be different six months from now, depending upon what has
happened in our lives. In the same way, we can understand how
the early church used psalms like this one to talk about the life,
death, and significance of Jesus of Nazareth.

In many laments, the psalmist's distress is likened to death, or
being overcome by the powers of darkness, or going down to Sheol
(pronounced shay-ole), also called the Pit. The Israelites believed
that Sheol was a region deep down in the bowels of the earth
where the dead, whether they were good or bad in life, existed as
shades of their former selves. Hebrew Scripture reveals no belief in
the afterlife in a Christian or later Jewish sense (except in the case
of Daniel 12:2–3, which is a late book, from the second century
B.C.E.).

The famous story of King Saul and the medium of Endor
illustrates Israelite thinking about Sheol. Saul asks the medium to
"bring up" Samuel, the prophet and judge who had anointed him
king, from Sheol. Samuel comes up as "an old man . . . wrapped
in a robe," none too happy about being disturbed, and gives Saul
bad news, reaffirming Adonai's rejection of Saul as king.

The psalms themselves are not all in agreement about whether
or not one maintains communion with God when one dies and
goes to Sheol. Some laments attempt to persuade God to act to
end the psalmist's distress by reminding God: "What profit is there
in my death, if I go down to the Pit? Will the dust praise you? Will
it tell of your faithfulness? [Ps. 30:9, RSV]" (see Psalm 88:6 below).
Death means the end of the relationship and of the psalmist's
praise of God. On the other hand, Psalm 139:7–8 insists: "Where
can I escape from your spirit? Where can I flee from your presence?
If I ascend to heaven, there you are; if I descend to Sheol, you are
there."

Psalm 88:3–6 offers an example of suffering described in terms of
Sheol and death. "For I am sated with troubles; I have reached
Sheol. I am numbered with those who go down to the Pit; I have
become like one without strength abandoned among the dead,
like bodies lying in the grave of whom You are mindful no more,

and who are cut off from Your hand." Is the psalmist actually dying? Perhaps not, since we hear words such as "*like* bodies lying in the grave," and "I am *numbered with*." Though the psalmist may not be on her or his deathbed, anything that threatens one's *shalom* (wholeness, integrity, relationship with God and people) is likened to death and makes one feel as good as dead.

Pastoral counselor Wayne Oates hears in the language of Psalm 88 the isolation of being trapped in an "iron cage of despair." Feeling helpless in relation to God and other people, the psalmist is trapped in a "can't do mode" and will not or cannot hear the good news of God's presence.[6] The psalmist feels cut off from God's presence and from the understanding of friends and family. The distress of the psalmist is deep in Psalm 88, and for this reason I used it in a memorial service for a young woman who had committed suicide. Those who had known her glimpsed the depths of her despair through the vivid metaphorical language of the psalm.

Psalm 88:6–7 moves into the "You" of lament language: "You have put me at the bottom of the Pit, in the darkest places, in the depths. Your wrath lies heavy upon me; you make me miserable with all your breakers." God is accused of causing the psalmist's present distress. That distress is described not only in terms of the Pit, or Sheol, but in terms of chaos waters ("breakers," "waves") overwhelming the psalmist. As Psalm 104 asserted (chapter 1), God has set boundaries for the chaos waters in creation. The psalmist of Psalm 88, however, feels as if those boundaries have been removed: she or he is experiencing the terror of the waters of creation out of control.

The Enemies (They)

The enemies in the laments are always vicious, and usually compared to mad dogs, bulls, or lions. The modern equivalent might be the pit bull. Psalm 17:10–12 describes them in this way: "They close their hearts to pity; with their mouths they speak arrogantly. They track me down; now they surround me; they set their eyes to cast me to the ground. They are like a lion eager to tear, as a young lion lurking in ambush [RSV]."

Who are these enemies in Psalm 17? Some scholars argue that they were false accusers in a law court or sorcerers or Israel's national enemies; but, again, most interpreters agree that we can't say who these enemies are. They are faceless enemies found in any typically human struggle, either national or personal.

When I posed this question about who the enemies are in this psalm to an intergenerational group at a church Bible study, parents were shocked to hear their teenagers say that the parents were the enemies in this psalm! Our parents, the youth felt, "don't really understand us," they "close their hearts to pity." "They track me down, lurking in ambush," always waiting for me to "mess up," to make a mistake so that they can ground me or say, "You see, I told you you weren't a responsible person." Some elderly people saw in this language a description of their adult children who were watching them closely for the first signs of senility. "They're just waiting for me to leave the stove on when I go out or forget my keys one more time, then, one, two, three, I'll be put in the nursing home."

Hospital patients saw doctors as the enemy in this psalm: "Just when I'm feeling a bit better, they order more tests and jab me for more blood; they hurry into my room, talk medical jargon and leave, never asking how I really feel or if I understand what's happening to me." Many people thought that their supervisors or bosses were like "lions eager to tear," waiting in ambush to deny them a promotion or a raise. At a pastor's retreat, the pastors chuckled with relief to hear that their colleagues thought of the pastor-parish committee or the church council or the consistory in this role—just waiting for the pastor to do something that they could complain about!

The description of enemies in Psalm 17 is one that most of us can concretize easily from our own experience. But what happens when we encounter the violent language of revenge against enemies in Psalm 58:6–8? "O God, break the teeth in their mouths; tear out the fangs of the young lions, Adonai! Let them vanish like water that runs away; like grass let them be trodden down and wither. Let them be like the snail which dissolves into slime, like the untimely birth that never sees the sun [modified RSV]."

Many people are disturbed by this negativism and violence. Brueggemann argues that in language like this "one speaks unguardedly about how it in fact is. . . . Israel does not purge this unguardedness but regards it as genuinely faithful communication."[7] The metaphors are strong and bold. If any of you garden, you are familiar, perhaps, with "the snail dissolving into slime." My garden in the D.C. area is plagued by slugs; an old remedy I use is to flick on the lights after dark and rush out with a salt shaker and sprinkle them, which causes their membranes to burst so that they literally dissolve into a pool of slime.

True, the psalmist does not ask for the personal power to punish enemies in this way; that is left to God, as is the case for all the laments except Psalm 41. Also, the psalmist asks that God take away from the enemies only what they use to hurt, that is, fangs, teeth. But these observations do little to diffuse shock over the hatred-of-enemies language in the psalms.

Some Christians believe that the God of the New Testament is a God of love, grace, and forgiveness and not the God of anger, law, and judgment in Hebrew Scripture; this hatred-of-enemy language, they hold, is not "Christian." But they draw an inaccurate dichotomy between the two parts of the Christian Bible, both of which show grace and judgment. A paradigmatic example of grace in Hebrew Scripture is in the Prologue to the Ten Commandments in Exodus 20:2: "I am Adonai, your God, who brought you out of the land of Egypt, out of the house of bondage." God's free and graceful act of the Exodus preceded God's giving of the law (the *torah*, the Ten Commandments). In Genesis, God forgives the matriarchs and patriarchs again and again, and works through their mistakes and doubts to keep the promise of land and descendants alive.

In separating the God of wrath from the God of grace, Christians point also to Jesus' Sermon on the Mount. "Blessed are those who mourn, . . . the merciful, . . . the peacemakers, . . . those who are persecuted for righteousness' sake [Matt. 5]." How can one hate enemies given this teaching of Jesus? In Mark 12:28–34, Jesus names the two great commandments: love God with all your heart, soul, mind, and strength and your neighbor as yourself. Where is there room for hatred of enemies if we are commanded to love God and our neighbor?

Yet the Jews of Jesus' time knew these commandments, too. The first is found in Deuteronomy 6:4–5: "Hear, O Israel, Adonai our God, Adonai is one, and you shall love Adonai your God with all your heart, and with all your being, and with all your might." This is the first part of the *Shema*, the supreme affirmation of God's unity, dating back to Second Temple times. The second is found in Leviticus 19:17–18: "You shall not hate your brother [or sister] in your heart, but you shall reason with your neighbor, lest you bear sin because of him [or her]. You shall not take vengeance or bear any grudge against the children of your own people, but you shall love your neighbor as yourself; I am Adonai." These two commandments stood in Hebrew Scripture along with the angry lament language about enemies.

Jesus is also quoted twice in the Gospels as saying "love your enemies" (as an antithesis to "hate your enemies," which is nowhere commanded in Hebrew Scripture) and "turn the other cheek [Luke 6:27–31; Matt. 5:43–46]." How can one be commanded to love? Even Jesus becomes angry; he curses a fig tree and overturns the tables of the money changers in the royal portico of the Temple mount. Perhaps the angry-enemy language in the psalms recognizes the difficulty of commanded love and speaks to the *process* of loving. Can we love someone before we acknowledge our hatred of him or her? Can such an acknowledgment of hatred be cathartic and diffuse a hateful action, especially if it is offered up in the context of worship within the community of faith?

Given these Christian protests against the enemy language of Psalm 58 and other laments, we must ask who the enemies in Psalm 58 are. Again, we cannot say for sure, but in a real sense they seem more than human. They represent all that is opposed to *shalom*, to wholeness, all that threatens life and order in the world. Since God intends life and order for God's creation, the psalmist's enemies become God's enemies as well. The enemies threaten not only the psalmist but also her or his God.

The urgency and vehemence of the enemy language in Psalm 58 comes, in part, from this identification that the psalmist makes between personal enemies, or the people's enemies, and God's enemies. Not only is the psalmist's future at stake, but God's reputation, too. Will God allow the enemies to triumph over the righteous ones who follow God? If God does give the wicked what they deserve, then, as Psalm 58:11 puts it: "People will say, 'Surely there is a reward for the righteous; surely there is a God who judges on earth' [RSV]."

The violence of the enemy language in laments also emerges out of the this-worldly focus of Hebrew Scripture. Because there was no life after death aside from Sheol until later in Second Temple Judaism (second century B.C.E. on, with the rise of apocalyptic literature such as the book of Daniel), injustices had to be put right here and now in this life. This was a matter of great urgency. Such a world view can, in the words of Roland Murphy, "serve to correct an exaggerated eschatologism [focus on the end time] which fails to meet squarely the realities of this life, such as issues of social justice, or the sacramental and wholesome nature of all God's creation."[8]

Erhard Gerstenberger[9] also argues that the theme of enemies and evildoers in the laments can help us to name social enemies, and thus relates to crucial social issues of our times. We must, in our impersonal world, be able to ask who is responsible for societal suffering and identify those who are guilty of destruction and dehumanization in our communities. We must show solidarity with the poor against existing power structures. The enemies in the psalm laments thus can become for us, as they were for ancient Israel, the structural enemies of our own society, supra-individual representatives of the chaos opposing God's good order for the world.

Rather than leave all our human problems to God to resolve in the end time (eschatology), or when we die, the lament-enemy language urges us to work with God now to transform and make new. We cannot dismiss wrongdoing in our life with a glib "Why should I worry? God will give them what they deserve when they die. She'll get hers; he'll get his." Rather than turn our backs on the world, the lament-enemy language pushes us to face the world and its pain now.

Although many Christians put this world's justice issues off until the next life, others do not even believe in a final reckoning when they die. In a recent newspaper article, Martin Marty, a church historian from the University of Chicago, is quoted as saying that before 1952 about half of Americans believed in hell. More recent surveys show that only 8 to 13 percent of Americans "thought of hell as in any way a possibility for them." Most, however, still think they are going to heaven when they die.[10] If not in this life or the next, then when will the wicked be called to account?

What hope is there for the oppressed? Why bother to be "good" at all?

The psalm laments insist upon an embrace of this life and a push to justice. Given what is at stake in the laments, it is no wonder that we hear angry and anguished calls for revenge such as we find in Psalm 137. Given lament urgency, we ought to shun any allegorical interpretation of this psalm that avoids its harsh enemy language. Many of us have been drawn into Psalm 137 by the haunting beauty of the opening words: "By the rivers of Babylon, there we sat down and wept when we remembered Zion"; the captors of the Jews in exile in Babylon taunt them to sing their songs of Zion in an unclean land. But we have also been repelled by the closing verses of Psalm 137, which are often omitted in responsive readings: "Fair Babylon, you plunderer, a blessing on [the one] who repays you what you have done to us; a blessing on [the one] who seizes your babies and dashes them against the rocks!".

In order to avoid this bloodthirsty language, some have read the psalm allegorically, seeing another and "higher" level of meaning beyond the literal one. Read allegorically, the psalm speaks of enemies in our lives that come to us at first as "babies", such as indulgences that are initially small, attractive, and harmless. Just as the infants of the enemy must be killed before they grow up to attack, so too must our "harmless" indulgences be destroyed before they destroy us.

What is most distressing about this allegorical interpretation is that it refuses to acknowledge the very real pain of the Israelites in exile. All of the symbol systems of Israelite life had been shattered by the Babylonians: The Temple had been leveled; Jerusalem had been burned; the king and the leaders, artisans, merchants, and teachers had been led away to captivity in Babylon. Those left behind to live amidst the devastation of Jerusalem and its environs were starving and homeless (see the Book of Lamentations). Yet despite this staggering blow at the hands of Israel's enemy, all that the allegorical interpretation acknowledges in the way of an "enemy" is our personal, little excesses that may grow to make us stumble. What an insult to the grief of the people and the depth of their pain!

Allegorical interpretation of Psalm 137 is a dishonest response, given the reality of the Holocaust and the oppression of whole peoples throughout the world today. Do we dare ask them in their suffering to deny their true feelings of pain and revenge? As Dorothee Soelle argues: "The more people anticipate the elimination of suffering the less strength they have actually to oppose it. Whoever deals with [their] personal suffering only in the way our society has taught [them]—through illusion, minimization, suppression, apathy—will deal with societal suffering in the same way."[11] We in the West erect walls between ourselves and the reality of suffering. We cultivate numbness, and so we are outraged by the intensity of pain in the enemy language of the psalms. The psalm laments do not bid us to share the sufferer's hate but rather the sufferer's pain by allowing that pain to be expressed.

Those who would suppress that pain forget a very recent time in our own history when we as a nation were outraged by our treatment at the hands of another country. When the Iranians attacked the American embassy in Tehran and took Americans hostage, many people called for the bombing of Tehran. Though we did not specifically call for the dashing of the heads of Iranian babies against the rocks, the net result of our bombing of Tehran would have been the same, dead women and children. How easy it is for us to condemn ancient Israel's cry for revenge and support our own, hiding behind our more impersonal methods of warfare! How many other times in recent history has America called for national retaliation in this way?

A pastor I know in Pennsylvania decided to embrace the anger and anguish of the enemy language in Psalm 137 during the Tehran hostage crisis. He used this psalm as the scripture reading and sermon focus on the Sunday after the storming of the American embassy. He told me that he felt he was taking the biggest risk of his ministry by doing that but that he could not conduct a worship service pretending his congregation was not angry. He did not believe that worship should force us to leave our real feelings, whatever they are, outside the church doors; that would not be an honest way to come before God.

The pastor preached his sermon on Psalm 137, pointing out how many of us felt like the Israelites, wishing for vengeance on the Iranians. He called upon his congregation to acknowledge and express their anger before God and then give it up on the altar to God. His hope was that through this communal cleansing, the congregation could redirect its energies to a different solution to the crisis. The vast majority of the congregation felt relief and thanked him for allowing them to wrestle with their feelings before God. They left the service with their anger acknowledged and diffused. How powerful a moment that was for them all!

This experience and the angry enemy language of laments like Psalms 58 and 137 raise the issue of the nature of spirituality. If we define spirituality as Brueggemann does, that is, "genuine communion with God," then the psalms remind us that "**communion with God** cannot be celebrated without attention to the **nature of community,** both among human persons and with God."[12] Psalm spirituality raises questions about the nature of the community, questions about theodicy. Theodicy is never simply a religious question about the character of God but is also a social question about life and the way we live it, about the struggle of the oppressed against the unjust, about a "**fair deal.**" The old "**consensus about theodicy**"[13] in Western society, which legitimated social structures as blessed and approved by God, is in crisis. It is being challenged both by Christian environmental awareness and by black, feminist, and Latino liberation theologies, which suggest different social arrangements in the name of the God of the exodus.

In this light, the psalms cannot be the private possession of those who pray them; they cannot be the stuff of romantic spirituality cut off from the world and the issues of justice. Psalm spirituality is all about the righteous and the wicked and the faithfulness and trustworthiness of God. The enemy language in laments articulates disorientation and the crisis in the ordering of life, not with violent acts but with violent speech, for "a new system of meaning will not come without abrasion, and that is what these psalms offer."[14]

The spirituality of Psalms 58 and 137 is passionate, but the psalmist does not take action and break the teeth of the enemy or crush babies' heads against the rocks. Because Israel leaves the vengeance to God, it can hope for a new Jerusalem. Brueggemann suggests that Psalm 137 might fit into Christian faith in the way it asks about how we endure and maintain identity. "This psalm poses some questions: Can there be a claim that overrides **forgiveness** for the sake of **constancy?** Can forgiveness be a mode of coming to terms too easily? Could it be that genuine forgiveness is possible only when there has been a genuine articulation of hatred?"[15]

Brueggmann's questions recall Dietrich Bonhoeffer's discussion of "cheap grace," that is, grace that lays no demand on us for obedience to Christ and moral behavior. This is "grace sold on the market like cheapjacks wares,"[16] grace without cost. Christian oversimplification of the sweeping grace of the New Testament tends to excuse our lack of moral outrage and acceptance of the status quo. Cheap grace asks no questions and sets no limits; all we have to do is leave the world and show up in church for an hour or two on Sunday morning, and we are assured that our sins are forgiven. This is as false a reading of New Testament grace as is the reading of Hebrew Scripture *torah* demands as excessive. Torah calls for covenant loyalty, for keeping God's commandments, for loving God and neighbor. Brueggemann's question puts both false readings in proper perspective: Can forgiveness be a mode of coming to terms too easily?

The Accusation of God (You)

In this part of the complaint, the psalmist accuses God of negligence or hostility, often by means of a string of harsh rhetorical questions. When enemy language and accusation of God are found within the same psalm, it is clear that the enemies are not the cause of the psalmist's distress; God is. The enemies simply make the situation worse.

As Brueggemann argues, psalm spirituality calls the world into question in conversation with God, a conversation that is honest and daring. Far from being unchangeable, "God assumes different roles in these conversations."[17] In hymns of orientation, God guarantees the old order and is praised for that. In thanksgivings of new orientation, God establishes a new justice. But in laments of disorientation, God is in the disorientation, absent or acting unjustly. This can be seen in Psalm 77:7–9, the first half of which talks about God in the third person rather than addressing God directly, perhaps indicating how painful the psalmist feels it is to express these questions about God: "Will Adonai reject forever, and never again be kind? Has God's *ḥesed* disappeared forever? Are God's promises at an end for all time? Has God forgotten to be gracious? Has God in anger shut up the divine womb-love?"

The verb "to forget" (Hebrew, *shakach*) occurs always in a question in the laments (Psalms 42:9; 44:24; 77:9; Lamentations 5:19). Psalm 44 contrasts the people's not forgetting the covenant with God's forgetting the people. In lament petitions, the psalmists ask God not to forget the one(s) praying. In the prophetic writings, God's forgetting is sometimes interpreted as God's judgment on the people for their idolatry and social injustice; God purposely ignores them (Hosea 4:6). In other prophetic passages, God's salvation is proclaimed as God's not forgetting (Isaiah 49:14–15). In the laments, God's forgetting is usually not associated with God's punishment but with the worry that the psalmist's problem has actually slipped the divine mind.[18] That worry probably also undergirds the petition in Psalm 44:23, a communal lament: "Rouse yourself! Why do you sleep, Adonai? Awake! Do not reject us forever!"

Psalm 77 mentions God's anger or wrath, but one should not assume that this divine anger is a deliberate response to the psalmist's sin. Often in Hebrew Scripture, God's wrath is not readily understood. In many lament psalms, no motivation for God's anger is given, for example, Psalms 6, 74, 88, and 102. Even in Psalm 79, which petitions God to forgive sins and deliver the people from their enemies, God's anger seems excessive—"How long?" Also, in the psalms "God's anger is never associated with beneficial chastisement";[19] suffering is *not* good for you. God's anger and punishment can be separated (Psalms 6:1; 38:1).

Many Christians are disturbed by such harsh questions as are hurled at God in Psalm 77; some call them blasphemous. Perhaps such Christians react this way because we all tend to want to pretty up our prayers before God, and we want other people to do so as well. We want to hide from God our true feelings of anger and doubt. We don't think that those emotions have any place in our prayer or in our relationship with God. Thus, when we voice our questions, we take on an extra burden of shame and guilt.

Our theology tells us that the things we fear—God's forgetfulness, inconsistency, or lack of caring—simply can't be true of God. Must we get our theology straight before we pray? There is a growing push today to let our prayer sometimes inform our theology: Begin with honest prayer and let it help us talk about God. As Pierre Wolff warns in May I Hate God? we tend to approach God "selectively" in our prayer and reveal to God only what we think God can handle; whereas, psalm prayer does not limit our relationship with God to "pious moments or sentimental hours."[20] If hate is our only channel of communication left open to God, then we ought to accept it and use it as Job did. God comes in the whirlwind, not despite but because of Job's angry words.

The psalmists risk encounter in order to keep up relationship with God. There is no false reticence in Israelite piety. The psalmists dare to speak to God directly and honestly. They think out loud in God's hearing. This thinking out loud may even involve angry enemy language and accusations toward God. This is intense prayer. God is not "boxed in" by this kind of prayer. If our relationship with God is real, "then God is open and vulnerable to being hurt, moved, and even changed by what [God's] children say and do."[21]

Robert Mcaffee Brown suggests that denouncing God in prayer is perhaps "a sign of how much we care, that we dare to express our outrage even toward the One who created us."[22] To be angry with God is not impious but an acknowledgment that God matters to us. The supreme insult would be to behave as if God did not exist by refusing any response. Though seemingly a strange affirmation of faith, Brown insists that the angry response is part of being truly human. This is expressed by one of Elie Wiesel's characters in his semiautobiographical novel of the Holocaust, Night, as he responds to the question "Why do you pray?" "A strange question. Why did I live? Why did I breathe?" Wiesel sees us raising ourselves toward God by the questions we ask God.[23] In a similar way, Wolff argues that our angry prayer moves us toward greater intimacy with God.

Harold Kushner evaluates anger toward God quite differently in When Bad Things Happen to Good People. He acknowledges that anger in situations of disorientation seems to be instinctive but that the important question is what do we do with our anger. Sometimes we turn our anger toward the person responsible, the one who fired us from our job, the spouse who walked out, the doctor who misdiagnosed an illness. We find someone to blame, whether or not the person is guilty. Sometimes the anger is turned inward as depression, and sometimes we are angry at God.

Kushner agrees that being angry at God won't hurt God; and if it makes us feel better, "we are free to do it." But our goal should be "to **be angry at the situation,** rather than at ourselves, or at those who might have prevented it, . . . or at God who let it happen."[24] Self-directed anger makes us depressed, anger at others scares them away from helping us, and anger at God "erects a barrier" between us and the resources of religion.

In Kushner's view, it seems there is little room for the angry psalm laments, even though for some, they are the only way left to God. This is because in reconstructing his theology in the aftermath of his son's death from a rare disease, Kushner relied heavily on the Book of Job and its discussion of suffering. Kushner argues that in Job three premises are laid out, which most of us would like to believe and which hold together when all goes well for us:[25]

1. God is all-powerful (omnipotent) and causes everything that happens.
2. God is good, just, fair and gives people what they deserve.
3. Job (substitute your own name here) is good.

When we fall into the pit of disorientation, one of these premises has to go in order for us to hold on to the other two. Job's friends wanted to throw out 3; Job got what he deserved, but he just didn't want to admit it. The friends blamed the victim. Job wanted to throw out 2; he protests his own innocence in chapter 31 and acknowledges God's power in chapter 42—what a blustering God assails him from the whirlwind in chapters 38—41!

Kushner wants to throw out premise 1; our suffering is not really God's fault. Kushner claims that this is what the author of the Book of Job believes, based almost exclusively upon one passage, 40:9–14: If you think it's so easy running the world, Job, you try it. In other words, God is still trying to overcome pockets of chaos in the world and is not all-powerful. In this light, Kushner's son's genetic defect was a random remnant of the chaos God has not yet overcome.

This theology brings relief to Kushner because if God does not do bad things to us, God can still be on our side when they happen and help us. This view frees God from our unrealistic expectations and allows us to be angry at what happened rather than at God, our enemies, or ourselves. We can feel God's own anger and compassion in the situation.

This is close to the stance that William Sloan Coffin adopted when his twenty-four-year-old son, Alex, died. His car slid off a dark road without guardrails into Boston Harbor. Angry over those who would claim that this was God's will, Coffin asserted in a sermon two weeks after his son's death that no one knows enough to say that: "My own consolation lies in knowing that it was not the will of God that Alex die; that when the waves closed over the sinking car, God's heart was the first of all our hearts to break."[26]

One cannot shake one's fist at this suffering God who is not all-powerful; one cannot pray the angry psalm laments. What happens to Jesus' last words on the cross in this theological view: "My God, my God, why have you forsaken me?" Such a prayer cannot then really be prayed.

Both Kushner's and Coffin's responses can be located within Richard Vieth's[27] categories of twelve theological responses to the problem of evil in the world. If omnipotence and goodness define God, then the presence of evil in the world forces us to choose between arguing that a good God does not exist or that evil is not real, since good and evil have meaning only as they stand opposite one another. If we reject both conclusions, then we may wish to attack the three premises listed above from which they are drawn, either rejecting or revising one of them to dissolve the contradiction.

Four positions reject or redefine the first premise of God's omnipotence: that the world is dualistic and evil forces vie with good ones; that Satan (leader of a domain of evil) exists; that natural order explains many events (thus, evil is a by-product of natural forces in an ordered universe; Kushner's view fits here); and that free choice, which includes choices made out of error, sin, and fallenness, is responsible for some events (Coffin's view probably fits here: his son "blew it" by driving too fast, although he may also argue from the perspective of natural order with Kushner).

Four positions reject or redefine the second premise of God's goodness: despotism (God is indifferent or malicious), judgment

(God punishes us for our sinful ways), testing (God tries our faith), personal growth (suffering leads to maturity, and, therefore, God wills it or allows it). Two positions explain suffering by denying or redefining evil: illusion (evil is not truly evil) and partial perspective (evil is real but contributes to a larger, harmonious whole, which we cannot see). Vieth lists as "additional positions" atheism (the reality of evil makes belief in God impossible) and mystery (we cannot solve the problem).

What do you think about accusations of God in the laments? Where would you place your own response to suffering and evil on Vieth's twelve-point chart? Where would you place the angry laments as a response to suffering and evil?

Petition

Petition is actually implied in the entire act of lamenting. The petition is a call or plea to God to intervene, to change the situation of distress and save the sufferer. The petition often uses strong anthropomorphic (human attribute) language, such as "Arise! Awake! Give ear! Answer me!" Implicit in these petitions are accusations of God: God is not doing what God is expected to do, and the petition, in effect, reminds God of this expectation. The petition is thus a call to both God's justice and mercy; these divine qualities are interwoven.

The intense distress of prolonged duration in laments calls into question individual and communal beliefs, or traditions, about God. The petitions name these beliefs about God and reflect how God has contravened them by permitting the distress.[28] In many communal laments, such as Psalms 44, 60, 80, and 89, God has not lived up to the traditional expectation that God is a God of holy war and conquest, who goes out with Israel's armies for victory and upholds the Davidic king. In each of these psalms, a foreign nation has victimized God's people. Psalms 74 and 79 lament the destruction of God's holy place, the Temple. Here, the Zion tradition (compare with Psalms 46 and 48) is called into question because God has not defended the Temple in which God is especially present with the people.

Thus the concluding petition of Psalm 44 pleads: "Rise up, help us! Deliver us for the sake of your ḥesed!" God is called upon to do what the tradition says God has done in the past (that is, deliver the people from their enemies in covenant loyalty) but which God is not doing now. In the same way Psalm 60 calls on God: "O grant us help against the enemy, for human help is worthless. With God we shall do valiantly; it is God who will trample our foes [v. 11–12]." Psalm 74 holds up the assaulted Zion tradition in this plea: "Direct thy steps to the perpetual ruins; the enemy has destroyed everything in the sanctuary [v. 3, RSV]."

In the individual laments, the complaints and petitions are more general pointers to the traditions being called into question by the distress. Usually the tradition most applicable is that God hears when called upon in prayer.[29] Prolonged distress calls this tradition into question and prompts anguished declarations like that in Psalm 22:2: "O my God, I cry daily, but you do not answer; and at night, but I find no rest." This state of affairs prompts petitions like that in Psalm 55:1: "Give ear, O God, to my prayer; do not hide yourself from my entreaty."

If the psalmist confesses sin, as in the penitential laments, the distress is considered to be God's just punishment, so the psalmist petitions God as in Psalm 51:2: "Wash me thoroughly from my iniquity and cleanse me from my sin [RSV]!" In Psalm 38:4 the psalmist confesses that "my iniquities have gone over my head [RSV]" and then petitions in verses 21–22: "Do not forsake me, Adonai! . . . Make haste to help me, O Adonai, my salvation!" In these penitential laments, God is the just judge who hears confession of sin so that one can be forgiven.

Very frequent in laments is the description of enemies who are making the psalmist miserable and of continuous weeping and groaning because of the enemies' actions. In these cases, God is called upon as deliverer to intervene and save, as in Psalm 80:2, "Stir up your might and come to our help!" or in Psalm 22:21, "Save me from the mouth of the lion [RSV]." God is also called upon to punish the enemies, as in Psalm 35:1, 4, "O Adonai, strive against those who contend with me, fight against those who fight against me. . . . Let those who seek my life be put to shame and disappointed."

Motivations

Laments often give God reasons to act to grant the petition, in addition to the very gut-wrenching descriptions of the distress given in the complaint. There are basically three kinds of motivation expressed by the psalmist to prompt God's action: confession of sin, protestation of innocence, or the reminder of the public relations value of the psalmist.

Confession of Sin

Most Christians are familiar and comfortable with the plea for forgiveness. Unison prayers of confession are standard in most Sunday liturgies, and they are lengthy, wordy confessions at that! The psalmist takes the blame for her or his suffering and says, in effect, "I deserve it, forgive and heal me, God," as in penitential Psalm 51:3–4; God is in the right. In penitential Psalm 143:8, 10, the confession motivation is contained within a petition for instruction: "Teach me the way I should go, . . . Teach me to do your will." Here the implication is that the psalmist hasn't been following God's way and doing God's will. The psalmist acknowledges this and enters a guilty plea in verse 2: "Do not enter into judgment with your servant; for no one living is righteous before you." If you evaluated me, I'd be guilty, God, so teach me how to do things right.

In the spiritual disorientation of these penitential laments, the psalmist's guilt is part of the suffering, as in Psalm 32:3: "When I kept quiet, my body wasted away." In verse 5, the psalmist confesses and God forgives; a new relationship is possible. Verse 1 makes that point up front: "Blessed is the one whose transgression is forgiven, whose sin is covered over." God is not blamed for the distress but rather acknowledged for merciful forgiveness. Enemies are often cited, and God is petitioned to punish them. But the enemies are not the cause of the distress; they simply aggravate it, as in Psalm 143:3, 9, 12.

The basis for the confession and plea to forgive in the penitential psalms is God's righteousness and faithfulness, not the psalmist's: "Adonai, hear my prayer; give ear to my supplications! In your faithfulness answer me, in your righteousness [Psalm

143:1]!" In Psalm 130, we have "the miserable cry of a nobody from nowhere. The cry penetrates the veil of heaven! It is heard and received."[30] The good news of the Bible is encapsulated here in that God's ear is especially attuned to cries from the depths.

The early church and the reformers preferred these penitential laments with their confession of sin to the more numerous angry laments, which do not offer any confession and in fact protest innocence. Because the church does not embrace these other laments, "one can say that in a certain sense the confession of sin has become the Christianized form of the lament."[31] It seems that sin has eclipsed suffering in Christian worship and theology. In this view, Jesus' work of salvation involved forgiving sins and eternal life, not relieving human suffering.

Thus, resistance to laments is undergirded by the belief that we should bear suffering patiently and not complain to God about it, that this world's suffering is insignificant compared to the guilt of sin. What is overlooked in this view is Jesus' compassion toward the suffering, his hearing of their laments, and his entering into human suffering through his last words of lament on the cross from Psalm 22. In the black tradition, Jesus acts as intercessor for our laments, reminding God to "remember how I felt on the cross?"

Protestation of Innocence

Rather than confess sin and admit that suffering is deserved, psalmists more often will protest their innocence, making it clear that their suffering is not justified and that they are therefore entitled to help. In Psalm 17:3, 5, the psalmist asserts: "You have tested my heart, you have visited me by night, you have refined me, you will find no wickedness in me; my mouth does not transgress. . . . My feet have held fast to your paths, by feet have not slipped"; similar is Psalm 26.

Many take offense at the self-righteousness that seems to be present in such a declaration. This reaction comes in part from our stoic acceptance of suffering without complaint because of our sinful nature (see above) and in part from our belief in act/consequence: You get what you deserve. We feel constrained to admit all our human sin before we can cry out to God.

But the protestation of innocence in the laments tells us that this confession is not always necessary. It is sometimes all right for us to express our pain in words if we do not honestly feel that our suffering is deserved. The lament protestation of innocence gives us a legitimate avenue of approach to God; and without it, we are left like Job, alone and comfortless on the dung heap, feeling wronged by enemies or abandoned by God. Without the lament protestation, we are left alone and isolated from God at a time when we need God most in our lives.[32] This can be extremely dangerous to our spiritual health.

The wider context of these protestations must also be taken into account. The Book of Genesis is filled with stories about the matriarchs and patriarchs who doubt God's promise and take matters into their own hands time and time again. Jacob, for example, is a scoundrel and a cheat. Moses in Deuteronomy reminds Israel that Adonai chose them, not because they were "more in number than any other people [7:7]" or because they were more righteous than anyone else (9:5), but simply because of God's gracious love. The prophets relentlessly point out the people's breaking of the covenant. The penitential laments declare, "No one living is righteous before you [Psalm 143:2]" and "If you, O Adonai, kept account of iniquities, Adonai, who could stand [Psalm 130:3]?"

Within this wider context of Hebrew Scripture, the anguished protestation of innocence is the emotional language of people in the pit of disorientation. It is language at the boundaries of life. As Brueggemann puts it, "The speaker has no time for theological niceties."[33] Perhaps, the psalmist says, "Given everyone else, I'm not so bad that I should suffer like this." The psalmist wants God to act quickly to overcome the distress; claiming innocence undergirds the urgency of the emergency call.

Public Relations Value of the Psalmist

Frequent in the laments is a confession of trust (see chapter 5) that maintains that God answers when called upon, as in Psalm 17:6: "I call upon you, for you will answer me, O God." Also, in the thanksgiving psalms (see chapter 6), the psalmist tells the story of how God actually answered, as in Psalm 30:2–3: "O Adonai, my God, I cried to you for help, and you healed me. O Adonai, you have brought me up from Sheol." Most psalms argue that if God allows the psalmist to die and go down to Sheol, then calling upon

God and God's answering are not possible, and neither is praising God for deliverance, as the psalmist does in Psalm 30:1: "I will extol you, Adonai, for you have lifted me up." Without deliverance God will lose the psalmist's praise; the loss is God's.

Thus Psalm 6:5 reminds God: "In death there is no remembrance of you; in Sheol who can praise you?" In Psalm 88, in which the psalmist feels very much as good as dead, there are several reminders like this: "Do you work wonders for the dead? Do the shades rise up to praise you [compare with v. 10; vv. 11–12]?" If, as we argued in chapter 2, human beings are always moving toward praise, then God robs them of their human purpose by not saving them from the distress carrying them to Sheol. "The speaker is **valued by God** as one who praises."[34]

Closely related to the motivation of the psalmist's value as one who praises God is the motivation concerning God's own reputation and prestige. As Psalm 9:16 declares: "Adonai has made the divine self known; Adonai has executed judgment." Similarly, in Psalm 10:13, the psalmist asks: "Why do the wicked despise God, and say in their heart 'You will not call to account'?" Implicit here is the argument that if God allows the wicked to prosper and overcome the poor, then God loses power and respect. The enemies in Psalm 28:5 "do not pay attention to the works of Adonai," the implication being that the psalmist does and that such regard is needed for God's power. The God who keeps order punishes the wicked in sight of all, as the psalmist in Psalm 31:19 argues: "How abundant is your good that You have stored up for those who fear You, that You do for those who take refuge in You, in front of mortals."

A corollary of this concern for God's reputation is the memory of God's salvation in the past, as in Psalm 44:1: "O God, we have heard with our ears, our forebears have told us, what deeds you performed in their days, in the days of old." The psalmist in Psalm 25:11 pleads: "On account of your name, Adonai, pardon my guilt, for it is great"; also Psalm 79:9, 10: "Help us, O God of our salvation, for the glory of your name. . . . Why should the nations say, 'Where is their God?'" God's reputation is on the line if those who call upon God are not answered. The present distress threatens God's reputation based on past deliverance.

The value of the psalmist's praise and the concern for God's reputation seem to some to be prideful human attempts to bribe God to act. Brueggemann acknowledges that "at times the motivation comes peculiarly close to bargaining, bribing, or intimidating. But this also needs to be taken as a kind of parity assumed in the relationship."[35] This parity can be empowering. It maintains implicitly that the psalmist matters to God.

We have now reached the "dotted line" within the lament structure outline. Something happens here. The tone and the language on the other side of the dotted line change from complaint to praise. Chapter 5 will examine that change and discuss the process of the lament. Several lament psalms in their entirety will be analyzed to illustrate the process.

Chapter 5

Life in the Meanwhile

The Process of Lament

The lament begins with address, moves into complaint, voices a petition, and offers motivations for God to grant the petition. At this point, one encounters the "dotted line" of the lament structure. Crossing over to the fifth point (see the outline repeated below), something happens. The mood moves from desperate urgency to trusting joy. The psalmist speaks in a surprising new way about God and the psalmist's relationship to God. Westermann was one of the first to notice this move from plea to praise. Brueggemann declares this move "one of the most startling in all of Old Testament literature."[1] Look at the lament structure outline again to see this shift.

1. Address
2. Complaint proper
   a. The psalmist's suffering (I/we)
   b. The enemies (they)
   c. God accused of not caring/doing (You)
3. Petition
4. Motivations
   a. Confession of sin
   b. Protestation of innocence
   c. Public relations value of psalmist
....
5. Confession of trust
   a. Usually introduced by *but*
   b. Faith that knows what it is talking about
6. Vow of praise

How are these two parts of the lament structure related, that is, 1, 2, 3, and 4 above to 5 and 6 below? How does the psalmist move from one emotion to the other? What is responsible for this move? What does each side of the dotted line tell us about faith?

Confession of Trust

The confession part of the lament psalm can be expanded to become a whole psalm of trust. Psalms 18, 23 ("Adonai is my shepherd"), 27, and 103 are examples. In the lament psalm, the confession of trust is an expression of confidence in God despite or in the midst of the situation of suffering. One participant in a Bible study I led likened the faith in the confession of trust to "the second wind of the runner."

The confession of trust is often introduced by "but," as in Psalm 55:16–18. This psalm opens with a petition, "Give ear to my prayer, O God [RSV]" and then moves into a description of the psalmist's suffering and of the enemies who taunt the psalmist. In verse 16, a shift in attitude is expressed: "As for me [but] I call upon God, and Adonai will save me. Evening and morning and at noon I complain and shout, and God will hear my voice." In the midst of the suffering and the enemies, the psalmist asserts the whole basis of offering up the lament in the first place: God hears, cares, and acts.

This is faith that knows what it is talking about. It is rather easy to profess trust in God when all is well. It is much more difficult and very painful to do so when the going gets tough and one finds oneself in the pit of disorientation. It takes a strong faith in God to keep talking to God, to keep up the dialogue, when our orientation is shattered and we are in despair. That is why the confession of trust is so powerful in the lament.

Vow of Praise

The vow of praise is not always found in the lament, but it follows logically from the preceding confession of trust. The psalmist vows in advance to thank God and declare to the community God's great act of deliverance on the psalmist's behalf, even though the deliverance has not yet occurred. Returning to Psalm 22, with which this study of the lament structure began, we hear the psalmist vow in verse 22: "I will tell of your name to my sisters and brothers, in the midst of the congregation I will praise you."

Some would call this the bargaining of a "foxhole religion"; we turn to God only when we are in trouble in order to strike a deal. "Listen God," we say, "you scratch my back and I'll scratch yours. Get me out of this mess and I'll make sure that everyone knows what You have done for me. I'll spread the word." How many times have we found ourselves in that kind of situation? Just let me close this deal at work, or let him recover from this illness, or let my wife come back to me, and I promise I'll go to church regularly and pray every day. We all try to strike these kind of bargains in our life of faith, don't we? When we do this, we are, in a sense, betting on God to come through for us. That God will come through for us is the belief that undergirds the whole of the lament and, indeed, all of our prayer.

If we believe that God is omniscient (all-knowing), then God knows what we will pray before we pray it. God knows we are betting on God to come through. Nevertheless, we have a human need to make sure that God gets the details right. Details are important. They help us to come to terms with our situation. That is why those who have just come through an operation are eager to give anyone who will listen (and even those of us who may not want to!) a detailed description of that operation: how long it took, what they took out and where, the length of the incision, the time spent in recovery, and so on. We need to hear the details of someone else's pit experience so that we can enter into the experience of the other person as sympathetically, genuinely, and dynamically as possible.

In the same way, God needs to know the details of our prayer so that God can act as sympathetically and as effectively as possible on our behalf. The confession of trust and the vow of praise in anticipation of the deliverance let God know what is at stake for God. In one way, the confession and vow function somewhat like the motivations (which, as we have seen, include confession of sin, protestation of innocence, and public relations value of the psalmist). But they are also declarations of the fact that the psalmist and God matter to each other; this is a statement of faith.

What has happened to turn the psalmist's lament into trust and praise in anticipation of the deliverance that has not yet occurred? Several explanations have been offered by scholars over the years, but we simply cannot know for certain. Perhaps some action took place that is not reported, for example, in Psalm 55 between verses 15 and 16, or between verses 21 and 22 of Psalm 22. Perhaps someone with authority, such as a priest, prophet, or elder at the sanctuary, heard the psalmist's complaint and in God's name declared through a salvation oracle that God has heard, go home and be confident. Perhaps God speaks through a priest after the lament's complaint and petition with words like those in Psalm 12:5: "Because the poor and needy groan, I will now arise, *says Adonai* [italics added]."

Perhaps this certainty of a hearing is more of an inward conviction on the psalmist's part that arises after the complaint has been voiced. The inner catharsis experienced by the psalmist makes the psalmist more receptive to the positive words in the fifth part of the outline, across the dotted line. Whatever happens to signal the change from complaint to praise, the movement within the lament structure expresses the normative belief in Israel that its God is "powerful and accessible" and is characteristically known to intervene to transform situations of distress. Israel's God is faithful to the divine promises; "saving reversal and not tragic reversal is the pattern" of Israel's experience.[2] Thus, a lament is an act of faithfulness.

Brueggemann sees Israel's whole history as a history of trouble and relief, lament and deliverance. This sequence is articulated in the paradigmatic exodus event (slavery to freedom); in the wilderness wanderings (hunger and thirst to manna and water); in the cyclical view of apostasy, oppression, repentance, and deliverance in the Book of Judges; in the story of the rise of King David to save Israel from the oppression of the Philistines; and in the public crises of the Assyrian threat in the seventh century B.C.E. and the Babylonian destruction and exile in the sixth century. It is this form of "cry and rescue" "which yields the boldness and conviction which results in gospel, that is, in good news."[3] In the same way, Jesus' actions (feeding, healing, forgiving, raising) are saving responses to situations of distress. The lament structure of cry-response was experienced by the early church as crucifixion-resurrection.

In the same way, Westermann sees the lament as witnessing to God's saving acts and deliverance. The lament is directed to the one who can deliver, and the confession of trust already anticipates that deliverance. The goal of the lament transition is praise of God, as seen in the vow of praise. In Hebrew Scripture, lament and praise are juxtaposed; "it is an illusion to suppose or to postulate that there could be a relationship with God in which there was only praise and never lamentation."[4] Something is therefore wrong if praise of God finds a place in Christian worship while lament does not.

The most important thing about lament is that the distress, whatever it is, is taken before God. God is believed to be the judge and redeemer, the guarantor of shalom (wholeness), the sovereign power over all distress. This belief is the ground for all laments. This means that our anger and doubts need not create a dead end for us in our relationship with God. We need not run around in circles of guilt for our honest feelings.

The basis for praying the lament is that God hears, that God is not defensive even when we lash out in anger. As Psalm 23 affirms, "Even though I walk through the valley of the shadow of death . . . you are with me [RSV]." God is with us no matter what we have to say, no matter how difficult the journey.

The laments are thus really expressions of praise and confidence in God when God is felt to be absent. This is the paradox of the lament and of our relationship with God. The very structure of the lament supports this. There is usually a consistent flow from the opening pouring out of troubles to God to a positive statement, from despair to praise. A lament is prayed precisely because there is faith in God's readiness and power to act on behalf of those who appeal to God. A lament, even when it does not move into trust and praise (as in Psalm 88), marks the human struggle never to give up on God, to enter into an ever-deepening relationship with God. A lament, as much as and more than praise, is insistent upon our relationship with God as crucial for our lives.

This insistence may give rise to expressions of harshness against enemies and God, but this harshness is really an expression of what

Pierre Wolff terms the psalmist's "desire for reconciliation."[5] Do we love God enough to tell all? Wolff argues that perhaps Israel's laments teach us today that we do not love God enough or believe enough in God's love for us.[6] Hatred is present perhaps "as long as people are mute; but as soon as they decide to express the anger that is in their heart . . . something is **already** changing and maybe even **already changed.**"[7] Love is already at work transforming us in the honesty of our speech. Wolff's argument calls to mind the main character in Herman Melville's novel *Billy Budd.* Having just killed a man, Billy says, "I woudna hit him if I coulda spoke." Our ministering to one another has less to do with running churches and serving on committees than it does with enabling communion with God.[8]

In the same way, Nelle Morton speaks of "hearing to speech," which belongs to women's experience, that is, hearing oneself to expression, or women hearing other women to speech. This kind of hearing is "a complete reversal of the going logic," a kind of "depth hearing that takes place before the speaking—a hearing that is far more than acute listening," a hearing that evokes new speech from the one heard. Morton contends that Pentecost was about this reversal: hearing followed by speaking. This kind of hearing is theological and revolutionary and has been "long programmed out of our culture and our religious tradition"; "hearing of this sort is equivalent to empowerment." We empower by hearing to speech.[9]

This kind of hearing that empowers speaking is revolutionary theologically because it counters "those theologians who claim that God is sometimes silent, hidden, or withdrawn *(deus absconditus)*, and that we must wait patiently until 'He' deigns to speak again." More empowering and realistic than this kind of silent despair would be our seeing "God as the hearing one—hearing us to our own responsible word."[10] This kind of hearing might challenge and negate the words of the theologians who have God all figured out. In this sense, God treats us as equals, hearing the speech out of us, in the lament.

We can learn how to hear the speech out of one another by giving permission to vent thoughts of lament and by allowing the entire process of lament to unfold. Dorothee Soelle argues that "the first step towards overcoming suffering is, then, to find a

language that leads out of the uncomprehended suffering that
makes one mute, a language of lament, of crying, of pain, a
language that at least says what the situation is." This language is
missing in our liturgies today. Modern day apathy has increased our
muteness; isolation and fear have diminished our communication
with one another. Communication by lament brings solidarity in
which change and liberation occur. "To become speechless, to be
totally without any relationship, that is death."[11]

The laments keep us alive and in relationship with God and one
another. They teach us how to go to the depths with the sufferer.
We give comfort to the one suffering by respecting the person's
right to lament, instead of censuring a lament as blasphemous or
unchristian. By allowing someone to express negative feelings
instead of making the person feel ashamed to express them, we
hear that person into speech; we empower her or him. We help to
keep open the disoriented one's relationship with God through the
only avenue of communication open to the person at the moment.

Some pastors have said in no uncertain terms that they do not
want to open such an avenue, that the lament process is not the
kind of example they want to set for their congregations. Others
have shared with me their own double bind on the lament issue.
Personally, many pastors yearn for the permission to express their
honest feelings in front of their congregations; they are human,
too. Yet how difficult it is for them to embrace lament language
knowing that some in their congregation would see this more as
weakness, as an inability to fulfill their pastoral role as example-
setter and moral model.

Many congregations put their ministers on a pedestal, and
neither the pastor nor the congregation wants the pastor to come
down. What a risk a pastor takes to be honest, to share personal
feelings with those in the church. A pastor becomes very vulnerable in this way. Is there room in your view of the pastor's role for
her or him to embrace the lament process? Should a pastor give
permission to us to lament? Consider this question in light of the
fact that Jesus listened to people's complaints and healed many
without censuring them.

It is cruel and dishonest to deny our real feelings and suppress
negative thoughts. Doing so is like saying that Jesus' death on the
cross eliminated all human suffering and injustice, which it did

not. We await the full realization of God's realm for that, and in this waiting we are not different from the psalmists. We have probably all felt as the psalmists at one time or another in our lives, secretly within our hearts or openly.

Think back in your own life to an experience of disorientation. How did that experience affect your relationship with God? How did that experience change your prayer? Did you pray angry laments? Why or why not? If not, what blocked you from appropriating the laments as a vehicle for your prayer?

When my brother died, I was very angry at God. Without the psalm laments, I doubt that I could have remained in the church and continued to teach in seminary. The laments kept me talking to God, even if all my talk was angry talk. There was comfort for me in knowing that I was not alone in my anger and my doubt, that the saints before me had prayed these psalms.

The whole process of the lament structure makes relief and healing possible. Simundson calls this the "power of negative thinking." It is sometimes necessary to work through suffering and doubt in order to maintain wholeness; otherwise, unresolved anger or questions can fester for years and eat away at our emotional and spiritual health. There have been countless times in my leading of Bible studies and retreats on the Book of Psalms, when participants have approached me after class and offered up their long-standing pain: "I'd like to share with you something that's been bothering me for six months. [One person had been angry over the death of her sister for over a decade.] I just couldn't tell my pastor. She [or he] wouldn't understand." How many times have you felt this way, isolated, angry, and ashamed? Perhaps I was the least threatening ear because I was a stranger. What a challenge to the community of faith to become that listening ear!

The structure of the lament reminds us that God is there and that God hears, even when our inner feelinigs have not yet caught up with this fact and when our sense is that God does not hear. When my brother died, I prayed the laments, but when I crossed over the dotted line into "confession of trust," it was only to mouth the words that as yet had no meaning for me. They were, at most, a dim light at the end of my tunnel, a light that I could not yet embrace.

What is crucial in this lament process is that we be careful not to skip over the complaint to get to the confession of trust too quickly. Most laments may end in praise, but we "cannot short-cut the process. . . . The agony will not go away by leaping immediately to happy thoughts. The resurrection comes only after the crucifixion."[12] This is why responsive readings in the back of hymnals that cut out the complaints of the lament are as good as useless. They are nothing more than what a person in one of my Bible studies called "pious pole vaulting."

The pastoral question for each of us becomes "how long?" How long does it take someone to cross over from the complaint to the confession of trust of the lament in order to embrace praise after a divorce, a death, or an addiction? We are usually too ready to speak a positive word too soon. Proverbs 25:20 warns against such a practice in its pithy wisdom way: "The one who sings songs to a heavy heart is like one who takes off a garment on a cold day, and like vinegar on a wound [modified RSV]."

Most mental health professionals today speak of the stages of grieving the loss of a loved one: shock (numbness); denial ("No, this didn't happen."); anger (at people and at God: "Why me?" or "How could you do this?"); bargaining (an attempt to postpone: "I'll change if you take away my loss."); depression (reaction to past losses or preparation for impending losses); detachment or withdrawal ("I just don't feel anything anymore."); acceptance or reorganization (time to get on with life).[13] These stages do not unfold in a neat, linear way; grieving is messy. How long this grief process takes is different for each person. It took me a full two years before I could in any way get a grip on my life again after my brother's death; for my mother it took perhaps eight.

In a 1987 University of Michigan study, up to 85 percent of the people who had lost a spouse or child in a car accident were still grieving four to seven years later.[14] In a 1985 report on bereavement, the National Academy of Sciences concluded that grieving affects one's physical and mental health. Connections between grieving and specific diseases such as heart disease were cited, as was suppression of the immune system.[15]

Unless we've been through a grief process ourselves, we tend not to understand why grieving takes such a long time. No less famous a person than Joe Gibbs, coach of the Washington Redskins, learned that when his father died. When the father of one of his reserve defensive backs had died, Gibbs said: "I couldn't understand why he didn't snap out of it. . . . I even talked to him: 'Clarence, your dad would not want you to lose your job'. So when Clarence came on the field to say how bad he felt for me, I said: ' . . . I want to apologize for last year. I could not understand the way you were. I can now'."[16]

Perhaps the best thing we can do when someone suffers a loss, be it divorce, death of a loved one, or whatever has shattered someone's orientation, is to listen to weeping, to angry questions, to bouts of depression, or to whatever else she or he throws at us. We need to avoid moralizing, lecturing, and theologizing. We need to pay attention to what Simundson calls the "survival level" of suffering, that is, God's presence in suffering mediated through us, rather than to the "intellectual level," which is concerned with reasons for the suffering.[17] It is easier for us to hand a sufferer a neat intellectual explanation of why he or she is suffering. That's what Job's friends did. Simundson argues that in the end, the message of Job is on the survival level, that is, "have faith," for there is no intellectual explanation for our suffering.

Yet, Simundson warns that we cannot simply tell people to "have faith," for that

> is to tell them to do something that they cannot do. You can no more order someone to have faith in God than you can order them to stop being depressed or be six inches taller or change the color of their skin. Whether or not we ever have the kind of faith that is able to endure suffering is not something that we can will for ourselves. If it happens, as it finally did with Job, or as it is structured into the lament psalms, it is a gift from God himself [sic]. Though we cannot make it happen, we can at least be open to the process that gives it a better chance of happening. That means that, even in suffering, we continue to address our thoughts and feelings toward God (as Job did) and that we be as honest and direct as we can.[18]

In this view, "faith" is not simply passive acceptance of whatever life throws at you; it is not simply the confession of trust and the vow of praise.

Faith also includes what comes before the confession of trust in the lament structure: anger, questions, petitions, and motivations. As Brueggemann puts it, each part of the lament structure reflects a real moment in our relationship with God. Each part has "its own appropriate time. But one moment is not less faithful than the other."[19]

Well-meaning people can point to passages in the Bible that talk about rock-solid faith that never waivers, but as William Sloane Coffin said of his fellow clergy, this only proves that

> they knew their Bibles better than the human condition. I know all the "right" biblical passages, including "Blessed are those who mourn," and my faith is no house of cards; these passages are true, I know. But the point is this: While the words of the Bible are true, grief renders them unreal. The reality of grief is the absence of God—"My God, my God, why hast thou forsaken me?" The reality of grief is the solitude of pain, the feeling that your heart's in pieces, your mind's a blank.[20]

How often do we use comforting words of scripture for our own protection from situations too painful to face? It takes courage to grieve honestly.

The lament takes seriously our uncertainty about God when we are in the pit. It is a response to God's hiddenness, which articulates that experience of hiddenness and brings it to speech. Our questions of Why and How long? are not simply preliminary to the confession of trust or the vow of praise. The agony and uncertainty expressed in the lament structure characterize "life in the meanwhile," that is, "life lived in the period between what has happened in the past and what is hoped for in the future"[21] in our relationship with God.

The lament uncovers the real doubt that emerges from the imbalance between the promises of God and the present situation. In this sense we can say that what is expressed in the complaint, petitions, and motivations (above the dotted line in the lament structure) represents life in the meanwhile, and what is expressed in the confession and vow of praise (below the dotted line) represents the past experience of God and the future hope.

Although past experience undergirds everything above the dotted line, there it is implicit only, overcome by the uncertainty of the present situation.

When too much emphasis is put upon the movement within the lament from complaint to praise, the lament is interpreted "less like a lament and more like another form of thanksgiving."[22] This minimizes the function of the lament as an articulation of our experience of "life in the meanwhile" and as a buffer against skepticism or atheism. The lament is directed to God with the expectation that only God can answer. Yet this problem in one's relationship with God is confronted within the religious community, so that worship keeps boundaries around our experience and our despair does not exceed our tolerance and destroy us.

Both the experience of God's hiddenness and of God's presence were integral to Israel's faith. As Balentine argues, faith in God presents us with the dilemma of God's absence and presence. The prophetic or wisdom view that righteousness signals God's presence and wickedness God's absence cannot always be applied. This discrepancy between the wisdom view and reality leads to questions of Why and How long?

Ultimately, the lament structure takes into account our human condition and our need to give vent before God to what we are feeling. Rather than trying to resolve the conflict between lament and praise or trying to synthesize the two, the lament structure holds them together in tension. "Doubt and despair are not mere side-steps in an otherwise optimistic faith. They are in fact integral to the faith experience."[23] The lament structure witnesses to a determination to hold together the premises: God is good; God is all powerful; evil exists in the world; and we are good. This is perhaps not as neat a situation as we would like, not a systematic theology, but it reflects the real experience of our life of faith.

Psalm 13

Psalm 13 provides a textbook example of an individual lament. It contains all the parts of the ideal lament structure. It is a clear articulation of disorientation. Something is wrong in the psalmist's life and in her or his relationship with God. There is no confession of sin to suggest that this disorientation was deserved. The psalmist is driven to doubt and questioning.

The opening cry in verses 1 and 2 combines address and complaint of the lament structure by asking the characteristic lament question, How long? a question full of reproach and accusation. The question precedes the name of God, as if the pain were so great that the problem had to be expressed immediately and abruptly: "How long, Adonai? Will you forget me forever? How long will you hide your face from me [1]? How long will I suffer pain, grief in my heart all day? How long will my enemy celebrate over me [2]?"

In these two verses, Psalm 13 uses a method of repetition that is found in many of the laments, that is, rhetorical, emphatic repetition of a single word or a brief phrase. This poetic form acts "as a kind of magnifying glass, concentrating the rays of meaning to a white-hot point."[24] This intensified structure identified by Robert Alter shifts our attention away from the repeated element "how long" to the material introduced by the repetition, the sense of God's absence, the grief, and the enemy. It is, however, the crisis in the relationship with God that is at the root of both the internal pain and the external problem with the enemy.

Alter argues that the repeated phrase never means the same thing twice. "How long?" is used four times in the opening two verses with increasing intensity and desperate urgency. Within the first line the repetition also moves the Hebrew poetry from the general to the more concrete and specific. The psalmist complains of being forgotten by God in verse 1a, and this is described more personally and concretely in verse 1b as God's hiding the divine face. This movement toward the personal can also be seen between lines; the general condition of being abandoned in verse 1 moves in verse 2 to the inward condition of the psalmist, who is burdened with cares and grief. Divine abandonment is also specified by the final "how long" of verse 2 as it introduces the enemy.

Desperation reaches a climax at the end of verse 2. The psalmist moves into the third part of the lament structure, the petition, with four commands addressed to God in verse 3: "Look at me, answer me, Adonai, my God! Give light to my eyes lest I sleep death [3], lest my enemy say 'I have destroyed him; my foes gloat when I totter [4]." The psalmist cries to God to "notice me, pay attention to me!" It is dangerous to accuse God of forgetting and turning away, but it is more dangerous to give up on God and remain isolated from God by thinking that this doubt cannot be expressed in prayer or worship.

The psalmist's call to God to look is meant to reverse the hiding of the divine face in verse 1b. God's turning the divine face toward the psalmist would mean that the psalmist's eyes would be lightened rather than closed in the sleep of death. The psalmist reaches out to God here, uncertain whether the psalmist's life really matters to God. It is this mattering to God that gives life meaning. That the psalmist mattered to God in the past is expressed by the naming of God a second time in verse 3a: "O Adonai my God." After the expression of the raw pain and doubt, the psalmist is able to claim a past intimacy with God and remind God of what they were to each other once. This claim of past relationship that seems broken now becomes the basis or context for the petition.

The repetition of "lest" three times in verses 3 and 4 complements the repetition of "how long" in verses 1 and 2 and stresses the danger and pain of the present situation. The phrases introduced by "lest" function as motivations for God to act. Death and gloating enemies mean defeat for the psalmist and for the psalmist's God. As God's public relations agent in the world, the psalmist by using these motivations wants to make sure that God knows what is at stake. The general complaint back in verse 1, about God's forgetting the psalmist, is intensified by the magnifying glass of reference to the sleep of death and gloating enemies.

In the midst of this painful group of motivations for God to act, the psalmist bursts forth into the confession of trust in verse 5: "*But* I have trusted in your *hesed;* my heart will rejoice in your salvation [italics added]." In the midst of suffering, the psalmist holds up the past relationship of covenant loyalty with God and the future hope of exalting God once again for that loyalty. God's loyalty will be expressed by saving the psalmist from the exultation of the enemies over the psalmist's death; God will reverse the situation so that the psalmist exalts God's saving work. The psalmist crosses over from the complaint to the confession of the lament structure between verses 4 and 5, holding in tension life in the meanwhile with life in the past and future.

Verse 6 articulates a vow of praise, which promises in advance to tell of God's deliverance when it happens (and the psalmist asserts it will): "I will sing to Adonai, because [Adonai] has done good for me." In this final verse, God is addressed, not in anger and doubt as in verse 1, not with intimacy as a claim on the past relationship as in verse 3, but as the object of praise, of doxology. These three different uses of the divine name mark the movement within the psalm.

Yet this movement ought not be seen as a neat resolution of the psalmist's distress. Broyles,[25] for example, challenges those who would see in verses 5 and 6 a granting of what the psalmist had asked God for, so that fear has subsided and the present distress is disregarded. To interpret the psalm in this way, we must assume that the psalmist drops each line for another. Poetry, however, enables us to see all the parts of the idea simultaneously rather than sequentially. Psalm poetry gives us synthetic pictures of experience. Psalmists hold onto each line until the whole poem is gathered.

This means that we ought not be too hasty to talk about mixed emotions or contradictions within a psalm. Different perspectives of the same experience are offered without any explicit resolution of apparent contradictions. This conflict may be the key to the psalm's message and to our own life of faith as well. In our fast-paced world with its shifting values, some of us would understandably like to pin the lament psalms down; we crave resolution and a quick fix. But the psalmists saw that the life of faith is more complex than that. Psalms give the church language that matches all our experience; our honesty before one another and God builds us up as the community of faith and the body of Christ.

Psalm 41

Psalm 41 could be called the Jerusalem General Hospital chaplain's psalm. It is another individual lament. With opening words of blessing from a priest for those who care for the weak, some see it as a ritual for the healing of the sick. Verse 13 functions as the closing doxology for Book I of the Book of Psalms. Instead of opening with address and complaint, Psalm 41 seems to express joyful gratitude to others in the congregation: "Happy is the one who is thoughtful of the weak; Adonai delivers that one from the day of trouble [1]. Adonai watches over and preserves them; they are called happy in the land. You do not give them up to their enemies [2]. Adonai sustains them on their sickbed [3]."

Yet in light of the confession of sin in verse 4 (which does not seem to have been accepted by God) and the lengthy complaint about enemies in verses 5–10, these opening verses are either a denial of the psalmist's true feelings or really a complaint. The irony is that this is the way it is supposed to be: God heals those who take care of the weak and protects them from enemies. But this is not the way it is now. The psalmist draws upon the tradition of God as protector, wanting to believe it; but the uncertainty of life in the meanwhile is too great. God is being accused here of negligence, of not delivering, watching over, keeping from enemies, nor healing the one who helps others.

Verse 4 expresses a confession of sin, but it is a historical account, a confession in the past: "I said, 'Adonai, grace me, heal me, for I have sinned against you'." The implication is that the psalmist should be forgiven, given the traditional beliefs about God just expressed in verses 1–3, but that nothing has changed. The psalmist has acknowledged weakness, but Adonai has not delivered, says the psalmist. Again, the act/consequence formula is being applied by the psalmist here: You get what you deserve. If I have sinned, then I suffer at the hands of my enemies; but since my enemies still plague me, you have not accepted my confession, God. Why not? Am I as wicked as my enemies? Just look what they do (verses 5–10).

"My enemies speak of me badly: 'When will she die and her name perish [5]?'" The enemies seem just to be waiting for the psalmist to die, like vultures. They seize upon the weakness of the psalmist in suffering by whispering behind [her] back: "And if they come to see me, they utter empty words, while their heart gathers evil thoughts; they go outside and speak them [6]. All the ones who hate me whisper together against me; they imagine the worst for me [7]."

Think about those times you have visited someone in the hospital, or when you were in the hospital yourself and people came to visit you. We are a bit timid and reserved when we visit a hospital. The smells, the routine, the atmosphere are very different from what we usually experience. Things are clearly not under our control there. As visitors we tend to hang back by the doorway or plant ourselves in the corner, taking care not to get too close to the patient in the bed. This, coupled with the fact that sickness and death are disgusting to many, contributes to an awkwardness. We just can't wait to get out. We check our watches to see when visiting hours are over. Heaven forbid we should sit on the bed or hold the patient's hand or get close to the sick one in the bed!

No matter how well-intentioned we are when we visit sick people in the hospital, in our awkwardness we make the sufferer feel as if there is something radically and inevitably wrong with him or her. When we are the sick ones, we sometimes feel worse after a visitor than before. Visitors often speak "empty words" because they don't know any better: "You look great! You look as if you could go home tomorrow." But we suspect that as soon as they leave the room, they shake their heads and "whisper together." What they really think is: "Oh, she looks just terrible! Looks as if she could die tomorrow."

To us as visitors it is as if the sick one has been taken over by something that threatens our own wholeness and health, and we want to distance ourselves from it as much as possible. Verse 8 of Psalm 41 puts this well: "They say, 'A deadly thing has fastened upon her; she will not rise again from where she lies'." Death and sickness are personified here as a dynamic power hostile to human beings. That's why we don't sit on the bed; whatever she or he has might be catching, might overcome us, too. The sick one is not whole or real, and is as good as gone, as good as dead. Even our trusted "bosom friend" sees us this way (verse 9).

Psalm 41 is the only one of the laments that asks for the personal power to requite enemies (all the other laments leave that to God): "But you, Adonai, grace me, and raise me up that I may repay them." For one who is suffering on death's door, the speaking of this wish for revenge against the insensitive ones may bring relief. The only power the psalmist has left is the power of words.

Verses 11 and 12 offer the confession of trust in the sense, perhaps, of forgiveness for sin. The psalmist knows that God is "pleased with me" by the fact that the enemy is not shouting, "Look, I told you, she was close to death. I knew she couldn't last!" and by a sense of being in God's presence. The wicked are those who live without God; they do not recognize their dependence upon God as the psalmist does. This thought brings the psalmist comfort, for no matter what else may happen in the psalmist's life, being in God's presence is the constant comfort. God's presence will not keep the psalmist from suffering but will help him or her get through it.

Communal Laments

Communal laments are not as numerous in the Psalter nor as usable for many of us as are the individual laments. Brueggemann argues that the category of the personal has become our contemporary mode of experiencing reality. With our privatistic inclinations, we've lost our public imagination. In order to gain access to the communal laments, "we need to think through the public sense of loss and hurt and tragedy that we all have in common."[26] I suggested in the last chapter that Psalm 137 lent itself to our public use in the Iranian hostage crisis. Psalm 44 is another communal lament that can articulate our public outrage. The problem with any of these communal laments is that they can feed our imperialism, a belief that we have been chosen to conquer other nations and set the world right, to our way. The communal laments also can substitute an "us vs. them" mindset for an honest critique of our internal dealings with one another in society. In this sense, communal laments are a double-edged sword.

Paul in Romans 8:31–39 quotes one of the verses from Psalm 44. A look at why Paul does this can help us to see how Psalm 44 can help us as a nation, not only to express our public hurt, but to work toward social critique and our own national transformation as well. On the surface, Romans 8 and Psalm 44 seem poles apart. The psalm complains to and accuses God, while Romans 8 affirms God's love and exults over Christ resurrected from the cross. A closer look at these two texts shows that they have more in common than just one verse of scripture. Both passages tell us something about what it means to have faith today. Psalm 44 represents our lenten journey; Romans 8, our Easter celebration.

Psalm 44 opens with a powerful hymn to God: "We have heard

with our ears O God, our parents have told us, what deeds you performed in their days, the days of old." Following this verse is a description of those divine acts in the past. The Israelite people take a long, collective look at their glorious history during the time of settlement in the promised land of Canaan. "God, you with your own hand [2]" drove out the nations for our ancestors so that they could dwell in the land.

But in the light of the complaint that bursts forth in the middle of the psalm (verse 9: "Yet you have rejected and abased us"), this review of Israel's salvation history is full of irony and bitterness. The memory of the past serves only to accentuate the agony of the present suffering of the people of Israel. Thus, the opening verse, rather than praising God, implicitly accuses God: You were once a God to be counted on, but where are you now? We in our present misery are sick of hearing about the "glorious" past.

How many Americans boast of our glorious history, not realizing that this history was one of oppression for many of our people! How many dream the American dream and find themselves shut out of it! Who can claim the ideals of a glorious past as operative right now, given the escalating homelessness of our population, the poverty of our children, the pervasive racism of our society, the drug epidemic striking at every socioeconomic bracket!

What situation of distress had provoked such despair, such anger, on the part of the Israelite people? Their present misery is described in a general way: "You have made us like sheep for slaughter, and have scattered us among the nations [RSV]." The community, perhaps in Babylonian exile, tries to shame God into action by asking in so many words, "What profit can you possibly get from abandoning your people like this? This is not good public relations for you." For the United States to claim its moral superiority before the world as a God-fearing nation, we need to get our own house in order. The rapidly changing world political and economic scene is causing our nation to reassess its role in the world and its treatment of its own people at home. This is the public crisis that may push us to embrace Psalm 44.

The people protest their innocence: "All this has come upon us though we have not forgotten you or been false to your covenant—nor have our steps departed from your way, that you should have . . . broken us and covered us with deep darkness [vv. 17–19, RSV, passim]." We do not deserve such treatment, Adonai. We don't know why we are suffering: "Nay, for your sake we are slain all the day long and accounted as sheep for the slaughter [22, RSV]." You are the culprit in our present misery, God. We suffer mysteriously because of you. Who in America can protest their innocence in this way?

This pain of Israel's undeserved suffering is poured into a harsh closing petition that very clearly accuses God of negligence: "Rouse youself! Why do you sleep, O Adonai? Awake! . . . Why do you hide your face? . . . Rise up! Deliver us for the sake of our *hesed!*" The people refuse to believe that God will not or cannot act, so they petition God with urgency and anger.

In Psalm 44, the Israelites struggle for relationship with God and won't let go. This is the point of the psalm, this not letting go of God despite, and in the midst of, our suffering, when God seems to be absent, not present to us. In Romans 8, Paul proclaims the flip side of our relationship with God: God refuses to let go of us despite God's seeming absence. We must believe that nothing can separate us from God's love in Christ: "If God is for us, who is against us [RSV]?" Christ is God's pledge to be for us, to save, to intercede for us despite the perils we encounter in our lives of faith.

"Who shall separate us from the love of Christ?" Paul asks. This is no rhetorical question; seven forms of trial are listed. It is precisely by quoting Psalm 44 that Paul seeks to show the difficulty of the Christian life of faith: "As it is written, 'For your sake we are being killed all the day long, we are regarded as sheep to be slaughtered' [RSV]." In light of these real dangers that Paul lists as assailing Christians, we must be careful not simply to sum up Romans 8 with the proclamation "Jesus is the answer." The problem of a Christian existence before God then and now is too complex for that. Paul saw that the pain of the life of faith is real. The psalmist also saw that the existence of the Israelites was painful when God seemed to be absent.

Both Psalm 44 and Romans 8 are saturated with experience of life in the world before God. Psalm 44's lament articulates the reality of "life in the meanwhile," the life of Lent, the period between what has happened in the past and what is hoped for in the future, that is, Easter. The faith statement undergirding Psalm 44 and proclaimed in Romans 8 is that God does not let go of us—

God is for us. This is Easter. But the reality of our lives is often that God hides, and peril assails us, and we must struggle not to let go of God. This is Lent.

Psalm 44, more than a hymn of praise, struggles to proclaim "God for us," even when the only words we can say to God are "for your sake we are being killed all the day long."

Chapter 6

I'll Never Be the Same Again

Thanksgiving Psalms and Enthronement Psalms

The lament psalms with their confession of trust and vow of praise anticipate the movement out of the pit of disorientation. Though each of us is different, so that we do not move neatly out of disorientation according to some set schedule, the hope is that we do move sometime into new orientation. New orientation is not a return to the orientiation before the pit experience. Having been in the pit we can never be what we were before the pit; we can never be the same again. Rather, we come to a different place on the circle, or the spiral, of the life of faith.

This means that the hole in my heart caused by my brother's death can never be filled by anyone else, not even by my son, Brian (who is named after my brother) or by my daughter Ariel. No matter how many times people tell me how wonderful it is that I bring healing with my study of the psalms, I would not hesitate for a second to trade all of that thanks to have my brother back, alive and with me in the world. The pit experience is never forgotten. It impinges upon the present and the future.

Perhaps life is more precious on the other side of the pit. New orientation, as a surprising gift from God, means that we can live with the pain of the pit experience so that it doesn't overwhelm

and incapacitate us. We can once again smile and rejoice over the
gift and beauty of life. We respond in awe and thanksgiving,
gratitude and wonder over such a gift; and we feel compelled to tell
the story of the reversal of our circumstances to anyone who will
listen. Just as we need to give the details of our pit experience to
help us deal with it, so, too, we need to share the details of our
climb out of the pit.

Brueggemann argues that the psalms of new orientation celebrate a new settlement of the theodicy issue, of the question of
God's justice and the ordering of the world.[1] The crisis is past, and
the psalmist or the community looks to a new stability and order
for life. Thanksgiving psalms speak of the personal experience of a
new order, while enthronement psalms speak of the public experience of a new governance. Surprises and newness overcome the old
way of looking at the world. This new way is inexplicable: "We do
not know how such a newness happens any more than we know
how a dead person is raised to new life, how a leper cleansed, or
how a blind person can see."[2] (Compare this with Luke 7:22;
15:24; John 9:25; and Isaiah 61:3.)

Thanksgiving psalms articulate this sense of newness and the
surprise of the movement out of the pit of disorientation. They
celebrate the gift of new orientation. Thanksgivings tell the story
of the past distress and of God's saving reversal of the situation. In
its form and content, the thanksgiving psalm is related both to the
lament and to the hymn. Like the lament, the thanksgiving is
both individual and communal. Also, we can say that the thanksgiving psalm is an expanded form of the thanksgiving already
present in many laments. Laments often, but not always, include
vows of praise at the end, following the confession of trust. After
the psalmist's complaint, she or he declares trust in God's future
help and promises to give thanks and to acknowledge before the
congregation God's anticipated deliverance from the problem.
Thus the lament often moves from complaint to thanksgiving.

There is one major difference, however, between the vow of
praise in the lament and in the thanksgiving psalm. The lament
vow praises God for deliverance that has not yet occurred but that
is hoped for and anticipated. The thanksgiving psalm, on the other
hand, praises God for deliverance already experienced. The praise
comes in response to what has happened, rather than in anticipa-

tion of what will happen. One is praise before the fact; the other is praise after the fact.

The psalms of thanksgiving were often sung during the offering of sacrifices in the sanctuary or the Temple. The word *todah* in Hebrew means vow or free-will offering, thanksgiving (the emotion or attitude), thank offering, thanksgiving sacrifice, or song of thanksgiving. *Todah* encompasses the concrete, external action as well as the internal attitude and intention. In Hebrew Scripture, the two are never separated; a person's actions must mirror that person's inner attitude. To offer sacrifices or worship mechanically, without the proper inner attitude of reverence for God, means that one is not whole, not healthy. How many times do we go through the motions of worship on a Sunday morning, without throwing our whole being into our worship, without having our inner attitude in sync with the sitting, singing, standing, and praying we do? How can we emerge whole from worship if this duplicity is the case?

The root of the Hebrew word *todah* means "to throw or cast." Therefore, *todah* can mean to set forth, recount, recite, make known to others. When we tell the story of our pit experience and of God's delivering us from it, we witness to God's action on our behalf. We witness to God's overcoming of the chaos waters, of injustice, of the enemies. As does the praise of the hymns of orientation, only more forcefully, thanksgivings give testimony for conversion. In telling our story of wonder and awe, we are evangelists, calling people to a life of faith in this God who has saved us. We share the good news, the gospel. One cannot, indeed, ought not, to do that lightly. The whole person must be involved. If not, God is perceived only dimly through us by others.

Hymns and thanksgivings share this evangelical aspect, of giving testimony about God. Both are addressed to God and to those in the congregation and the world. Yet there is an important difference between them. The hymn praises God in general terms as one who creates the world, deals graciously with people, gives refuge in troubled times, and so forth. Hymns in this way focus upon who God is. It is God's nature to be gracious, to save, to hear prayer; and this nature is revealed to us constantly. This focus upon God's general nature is reinforced by the use of active participles to talk about God: "the one who continuously does . . ."

In the thanksgivings, however, the "I" of the psalmist is often the subject and the verbs are finite, in the past tense. The stress is upon the event from which God rescued "me"; for example, God rescued *me* from the Pit; God did not let *my* enemies rejoice over *me*. Whereas God *acted* in the thanksgiving, God *is* in the hymn. Thanksgivings give more specific and concrete praise of God than hymns, but sometimes it is difficult to decide if hymns and thanksgivings express orientation or new orientation. In these cases, who uses them and how she or he uses them will determine which movement of faith is being expressed.

The Structure of the Thanksgiving Psalm

Like the hymn, the thanksgiving can be broken down form-critically into three parts: (1) introduction, (2) body, and (3) conclusion. In the introduction, praise and thanks are usually combined in an opening declaration or call to others to join in. The body presents the story of the individual giving thanks. A picture is drawn of the past distress and the psalmist's cry for help. The same metaphorical language we saw in the study of laments is present in this section of the thanksgiving psalm; it makes sense that lament motifs appear in this middle section. Often English translations will use quotation marks to indicate that these are the psalmist's very words from the pit during the time of distress.

Describing the pit experience helps to underscore the deliverance that God has brought about. In keeping with this emphasis on deliverance, the psalmist clearly acknowledges God as the deliverer; no one else but God could have done this for the psalmist. Often this acknowledgment is expanded into instructions for bystanders. Take heed of my experience, the psalmist says; join with me in praise for the God who has done this for me and will do the same for you.

In the conclusion, the psalmist returns to the introductory theme of praise and thanksgiving. Sometimes the opening words will be repeated. Because rescue from the pit does not mean that the psalmist will never again experience distress, the psalmist will often add a prayer for future help: If I should find myself in this situation again, God, listen to me again and deliver me; don't think I don't need you anymore. This prayer for future help articulates the psalmist's real sense of dependence upon God. Having been in the pit drives that point home.

Psalm 30

Communal psalms of thanksgiving include Psalms 65, 67, 107, and 124; individual thanksgivings include Psalms 18, 30, 92, 103, 116, and 138. Psalm 30 presents us with a compact model of a thanksgiving psalm. Though the psalm is used at Hannukah, the festival of the rededication of the temple in the second century B.C.E., this was probably not its original use. Israel's memory of the transformation of its pit of foreign oppression to freedom under the Maccabees is part of Israel's pattern of experience with its God of transformation, but this pattern was experienced and testified to by individuals, too.

Psalm 30 opens with the praise declaration: "I will extol you, Adonai," and moves immediately to the body, or story of the past distress, in verse 1b: "For you have drawn me up and have not let my enemies rejoice over me." Verses 2 and 3 continue the story of the past distress with metaphorical language, frequent in the laments: "O Adonai my God, I cried to you for help and you healed me. O Adonai, you brought me up from Sheol, you kept me from going down into the Pit." God, the transformer of situations, reversed the psalmist's situation of distress. The verbs underscore this reversal: You drew me *up* [verse 1b] and brought me *up* [verse 3a] rather than let me go *down* to the Pit [verse 3b, italics added].

The phrases "I cried" and "you healed" in verse 2 also stress God's transformative deliverance. The cry stands at the center, between the two verbs of movement up and out of distress. The cry is the reality of the pain of the pit, which is enveloped and surrounded both theologically and structurally in these verses by God's saving actions. Each of us can concretize what it has meant in our own lives to be enveloped in this way, to be brought up from Sheol, to be healed by God, the transforming One.

The cry also speaks of intimate relationship. God is addressed three times in these first three verses. The second time, in verse 2,

God is not simply addressed as Adonai, as in verses 1 and 3, but as "Adonai *my* God." This is an address of intimacy, claiming a past relationship and asserting at the same time the renewed relationship of the present, post-pit experience. This claim is also enveloped by the saving actions of God. The foundation of the lament is the belief that God answers prayer and hears cries of distress. This belief is confirmed and upheld by verses 1b–3.

The wonder of this deliverance as an answer to prayer pushes the psalmist to issue a sweeping call to praise in verse 4, because this good news cannot be kept secret, cannot be stored up as a personal treasure. The psalmist must testify about the God who has done this and must call others to join in the testimony (verse 4): "Sing praises to Adonai, God's covenant loyal ones, and give thanks to God's holy name." In the same way, Psalm 40:9–10 expresses this compulsion to evangelize: "I have announced [your] righteousness in a great congregation; see, I did not close my lips; I have not hidden your saving help within my heart, . . . I have not concealed your *hesed* and your faithfulness from a great congregation."

Verses 4 and 5 constitute a mini-hymn of their own within Psalm 30. Verse 4 would be the opening call to praise and verse 5 the reason for the praise, or the body of the hymn: "For [God's] anger is but for a moment, and when God is pleased there is life. Weeping may linger for the night, but joy comes with the morning." In verse 5, the psalmist generalizes about the life of faith and the character of God from the personal experience of God's reversal. Real pain (God's anger and the weeping it causes) is acknowledged in the life of faith, but it is seen as temporary. God's favor overcomes our pain, and joy follows. This is the good news, the gospel, that the psalmist must share. What else can we as saved creatures do but testify to the saving work of such a God?

God's grace can be seen in the divine anger that does not last. God's favor is what endures. Weeping is not the last word with the God of grace who reverses situations of distress. Here the psalmist gives instruction about God's nature to those hearing the story. Out of the personal and specific deliverance of the psalmist, the whole community is summoned to praise this God of grace. Thus Brueggemann argues, "As the psalm moves from reason to summons, so songs of thanksgiving move from intimate, personal experience to comprehensive, communal celebration."[3]

The psalmist in verse 4 addresses the *hasidim,* poorly translated in many English language Bibles as "saints." This noun is related to the word *ḥesed*, which we have seen used so often in the psalms for God's covenant loyalty. The *hasidim* are those within the community of faith who keep covenant, who follow in the paths God has set out for them, who keep *torah*. These are the ones who would understand and value the marvelous transformation in the life of the psalmist that has just occurred. The *hasidim* as a distinct group emerged in the time of the Maccabees, in the mid-second century B.C.E., to maintain their Jewish identity in the face of death and foreign coercion. Some scholars argue that the *hasidim* were the forerunners of the Pharisees of Jesus' time. This can be a sobering corrective to the very negative and biased pictures of the Pharisees in the gospels.

The psalmist resumes the story of the past distress in verse 6, offering a more concrete picture of what happened through the actual words spoken during the time of disorientation. Actually, the psalmist begins with the time of orientation, quoting the motto we have seen in hymns of orientation (such as Psalm 46): "As for me, I said in my unconcern [my ease], 'I shall never be shaken [or totter]'." The psalmist reveals that she or he never thought the pit was a possibility; everything was under control and secure. What the psalmist didn't realize was that the security and order was dependent upon God. The realization comes in verse 7: "For you, O Lord, when you were pleased, set me up as a strong mountain. When you hid your face, I was terrified."

The movement out of orientation into disorientation is described here in verses 6 and 7. The pain of life in the meanwhile gives rise to supplication and rhetorical questions in verses 8–10, which are meant to motivate God to act: "To you, Adonai, I cried and to Adonai I made appeal: 'What profit is there in my death, if I go down to the Pit? Can dust praise you? Will it tell of your faithfulness? Hear, Adonai, and grace me! Adonai, be my helper!'"

The memory of the very words said make the pit experience real again for the psalmist and for those who hear the psalmist's story. The rhetorical questions remind God of the psalmist's public relations value in the world. At the same time, those words remind the ones listening of their duty to praise the God who gives them being.

Verses 11–12a provide a summary of the situation of transformation: "You have turned my mourning into dancing for me; you have thrown off my sackcloth and clothed me with joy, so that my whole self might sing praises to you and not be silent." The psalmist ends the body of the thanksgiving, the story of the deliverance, with a statement of reversal: mourning into dancing, sackcloth into joy clothes.

The same verb, "sing praises," used in verse 12a is used in verse 4 in the call to the faithful to join the psalmist in singing praises. In verse 1b, God did not allow the psalmist's enemies to rejoice over the psalmist; in verse 11, the same verb, "rejoice," is now used of the psalmist. The psalmist is literally clothed in rejoicing because of the deliverance God has carried out. The psalmist concludes in verse 12b with a declaration echoing the opening line, but now reinforced by the story of the reversal: "O Adonai, my God, I will give thanks to you for ever." The psalmist claims an intimate relationship with God here, not as a motivation for God to act to pull the psalmist out of the pit, but as an acknowledgment that this has already happened, that God is indeed one to be counted on, now and in the future.

What is most powerful about this thanksgiving psalm is the way in which it lays out the story of a personal deliverance as the stuff of communal celebration for the faithful. How often do our personal stories become the catalyst for communal celebration in our liturgies? Sadly, we have managed to standardize and tame our personal stories of liberation or healing. We tuck away our excitement in general announcements before the call to worship or in the pastoral prayer: "So and so is recovering from her operation at home; little Johnny is recovering from his broken leg and we are grateful." There is usually no place within the Sunday service for our personal testimonies to God's actions on our behalf. We can pray our thanks silently, but we miss the communal dimension of thanksgiving when we do.

Why are we so timid about our good news? Even Mary Magdalene and the other women were afraid when they discovered the empty tomb, the greatest reversal of all; but they went out and told the disciples what they had seen. Because the psalm thanksgivings keep the memory of pit experiences and of God's rescue fresh, "each time they are sung, they invite Israel to participate in that entire history of transformation again."[4] Brueggemann insists that this participatory quality guards against the idolatry of an un-changeable God and an ideology of an unchangeable world. Thanksgivings can keep us, as they kept Israel, open to newness and transformation if we but take the risk and share them. Have we opted, instead, for control and safety in our liturgies as a protection against surprises and the newness of God's transforming power?

Psalm 47

Another psalm type that expresses new orientation is the enthronement psalm, also called the hymn to God the sovereign. Even though form-critically this type of psalm is a hymn, not all hymns express new orientation. Enthronement psalms emerge naturally out of Israel's claim that its God is supreme as Creator of the whole earth (Psalm 104) and is especially enthroned in Zion (Psalms 46 and 48). It makes sense that Israel would also claim that its God is sovereign over all the world and over other gods and peoples of the world.

Something new happens in the enthronement hymns, if we take them seriously as instruments of what Brueggemann calls "world-construction" in our liturgies.[5] Our worship not only directs our praise to heaven as a response to God but also constitutes a social act that shapes human community and the commitments we make in the world. The alternative community that emerges from the liturgical process is in tension with other kinds of community already in existence, because it is shaped by the character of Adonai.

Mowinckel argued that for Israel, the central liturgical act is the enthronement of Adonai as sovereign. The enthronement psalms construct a world over which Adonai rules, a world that challenges all other known worlds. Our use of the enthronement psalms in Christian liturgy today can challenge us, too, to create an alter-native community in which Jesus Christ is truly sovereign.

Enthronement psalms include Psalms 47, 93, and 96 through 99. Psalm 47 surfaces the essential features of the type. It begins as other hymns we have seen, with an introductory call to praise in verse 1: "All you peoples, clap your hands! Shout to God with the sound of joyous shouting!" The call to praise is sweeping; "all peoples" are addressed, not just Israel, and they are to clap and shout with joy. Weiser notes how the clapping is an appropriate response to this world Sovereign; it is "a thunderous echo of the divine might."[6] Everyone is called upon to acknowledge God's sovereignty, which is not seen as oppressive or burdensome but as cause for celebration.

The body of the hymn begins in verse 2 and continues through verse 4, presenting the reasons for the praise: "For Adonai Most High is awesome, a great sovereign over all the earth." The scope of verse 2 is universal, as is verse 1: God reigns over "all the earth." Adonai Most High in Hebrew is Adonai Elyon. Elyon is the high god of the Jebusites, a Canaanite people of pre-Davidic Jerusalem. Israel's God takes over Elyon's functions and characteristics. In this sense we can see how the enthronement psalms are perhaps derived from songs that celebrate Israel's victory over its enemies (for example, Exodus 15 and the Song of Miriam celebrate the defeat of the pharaoh and his Egyptian army). *Elyon* is used frequently in Hebrew Scripture where foreign peoples, in addition to the Israelites, are present.[7] In the same way, Christian doxologies and the Gloria Patri ("Glory be to the Father") express our claims for the victory of our God over all the others.

In verses 3 and 4, reference is made to the saving history of God's actions on Israel's behalf, during the settlement in Canaan: "Adonai subdues peoples under us, and nations under our feet. Adonai chooses our heritage for us, the pride of Jacob whom Adonai loves." Israel is chosen, elected by God to a special relationship with God, who carries out mighty acts for its sake. Israel's heritage is the Promised Land, which has been taken from the people already in it; these subjugated "peoples" are called upon in the opening verse (the same noun is used) to clap and shout in joy to Adonai.

Yet, lest we think that this is simply a psalm that rubs salt into the wounds of the subjugated people and legitimates Israel's oppression of them, we must look more closely. Israel's election is a function of the grace of this awesome God who is sovereign over all the earth. It is this grace that undergirds the call to praise. The focus in verses 1–4 is on God, not Israel. There is no hint that

Israel is to dominate the gentile nations in the future. The end of the psalm makes this very clear, as we shall see.

Verses 5–7 form their own little liturgical section. They seem to indicate that some cultic drama or procession is taking place. Verse 5 declares: "God has gone up with a shout, Adonai with the sound of a trumpet." Perhaps the Ark of the Covenant, the invisible throne of God and symbol of God's presence in battle, is being carried in procession to the sanctuary or Temple. The verb used for God's going up, *alah,* is a technical term for the pilgrimage to Jerusalem or the holy place of worship. God has gone up to take God's rightful place as the end goal of the peoples' pilgrimage; the sovereign of all the earth is to be worshiped by all the peoples of the earth. How appropriate that early Christianity used Psalm 47 as one of the psalms for Ascension Day.

The cultic declaration in verse 5 is followed by a mini-hymn for the processional in verses 6 and 7. The call to praise in verse 6 commands: "Sing praises to God, sing praises! Sing praises to our sovereign, sing praises!" The body or motive for the praise is offered in verse 7a: "For sovereign of all the earth is God." Verse 7b concludes with a renewed call to praise: "Sing praises with a psalm!" The use of "sovereign [*melek*] over all the earth" in verses 2 and 7 ties the two sections of the psalm together. The peoples in verse 1 shout "with the sound of joyous shouting" while in verse 5, God goes up with a shout.

The heart of the psalm, and the possibility for new orientation, is found in the declaration of verse 8: "Elohim *malak* over the nations; God sits on [God's] holy throne." The first half of the verse is translated in many different ways: "God reigns over the nations"; "God has become sovereign over the nations"; "God has always reigned over the nations"; "God has just now become sovereign over the nations." (The other enthronement psalms use Adonai [LORD], Israel's special name for God, instead of Elohim [God].)

The emphasis in this psalm is most probably not on God's continuing reign as sovereign but rather on the action of this moment, when God just now becomes sovereign. This is what liturgy is, not just a recollection or remembering, but a making so, "an enactment of a fresh drama in this moment."[8] This is news, not merely the repeating of what has always been the case. The claim of verse 8 becomes real at this moment in the liturgy; it is genuinely new. God begins a new reign.

The news must be experienced, not simply affirmed. To sing "Christ the Lord is risen today" on Easter Sunday morning is to make it so, to begin a new part of the liturgical year, to orient ourselves anew in the world. The church's liturgy dramatizes this new world here and now. At Christmas, which Brueggemann calls the festival of enthronement, we sing "Joy to the world! the Lord is come. . . . the Savior reigns"; the church enacts Jesus' coming to power in this very moment.

Brueggemann warns that "this dramatic enactment is not game playing"; rooted in memory, this "fresh announcement" changes the world.[9] It is the announcement that evokes from us new ways of being in the world. Brueggemann suggests that one can see the same dynamic at work in our experience of the death of a loved one. The death has no significance until the news is told. I remember that to be the case when my brother died. In my denial, I could not accept the news until I started telephoning the relatives to tell them what had happened. After about the fifth call, his death became more real to me, and I set about making arrange-ments for bringing his body home.

Because it is Adonai who has come to reign just now over all the earth, the earth is presented with the possibility just now of reflecting this divine character. In Psalms 96, 98, and 99, Adonai is great and judges the peoples with equity and righteousness. In Psalm 97, Adonai preserves and delivers the covenant loyal ones (hasidim). This is good news and a source of joy. "All the earth" is called to "sing a new song" to Adonai and shout with joy in these enthronement psalms, for the world can now take on this divine character of righteousness and faithfulness.

In Psalm 47, God is awesome, the one who subdues; and "the shields of the earth" belong to this God (verse 10). The "shields of the earth [2 Chron. 12:9–10]" represent the earthly forces of war, symbols of political power, the subjugation of one people to another. All these belong to God and are not available to humankind. Here is a great eschatological picture of peace, much like that sketched in Psalm 46:8–9, in which God "makes wars cease to the ends of the earth, breaks the bow, and shatters the spear" and proclaims "I am exalted!" So, too, does the psalmist end Psalm 47 with the declaration that "God is highly exalted!"

This vision of peace is the possibility that the shout "God has just now become sovereign" holds out to the peoples of the earth and especially to Israel. This is the new world that can be set in motion by the liturgy of God's enthronement. Not only will peace reign in this newly constructed world, but distinctions will also be erased, as a careful reading of verse 9a reveals: "The princes of the peoples are gathered together, the people of the God of Abraham."

The Hebrew text is elliptical; it lacks the word *as* or *with,* which most English translations supply between the words *together* and *the people.* Note that the leaders of the peoples are not called *sovereigns,* because only God deserves such a title. These peoples do not become part of the people of Israel, which would imply that Israel had subjugated them: "The princes of the people are gathered together as the people of the God of Abraham." Instead, the relationship between them and Israel is left ambiguous, full of possibilities in this newly constructed world enacted in liturgy.

In this eschatological picture (the picture of the end time), Israel and all the world's peoples worship the God to whom they all belong. The present oppressive structures of the world are challenged by the announcement of God's universal rule. "All who share the dramatic moment of announcement and celebration are energized to live in this new world with these fresh possibilities . . . therefore the world can act out its true character as God's creation."[10] What would that mean for our world today if we were to acknowledge God's universal rule? How radically different our political structures would be! "Globalization" would become real, rather than the abstract term it is for many. What stands in the way of our realizing the possibilities held out by the enthronement psalms? The answers include fear of people different from us, national pride, greed, thirst for power, and ignorance.

The social liberation thrust of what Brueggemann calls the **"slave memory"** of the exodus stands in tension with the **"grand claims"** of the Jerusalem liturgy supervised by the king in the enthronement psalms.[11] The enthronement liturgy reflects the royal establishment and serves the status quo of the Temple complex, Jerusalem politics, and the Davidic dynasty. The king is in charge of this liturgy and manages it. This control can work against the transformation possible in the enthronement liturgy. Therefore, to proclaim "God reigns" or "Adonai reigns" will have a different effect depending upon who announces it, hears it, and believes it. The slave will hear hope; the upper class worshipers in Solomon's temple will hear a threat. What do we hear on Sunday mornings? What do we mean when we sing "Christ the Lord has risen today" on Easter Sunday?

Although the king as "participant, sponsor, and benefactor" of the enthronement festival shapes the liturgy, thereby controlling it, the king as "**creature, child,** and **heir**" of the liturgy will be shaped by it, critiqued by it, challenged by it. The king can submit to the liturgy and embrace the world of justice and righteousness that liturgy creates, not the world of royal power. The king has choices to make concerning his own rule in Jerusalem in light of God's universal rule. The king can choose to do on earth what God does in heaven. (Isn't this the choice we can make each time we pray "Thy kingdom come, Thy will be done, On earth as it is in heaven"?) Do we simply mouth words, not realizing what is at stake? "The praise of Israel is not done in a social vacuum. . . . Praise is the beginning of political practice."[12] Do we worship on Sunday morning in a social vacuum, or do we allow the liturgy to create for us social, political, and economic possibilities? Do we worship to escape the world or to embrace it? If we use the enthronement psalms in our liturgy, we open ourselves, our world, and the way we run our world to critique and transformation. Liturgy and worship are risky business. Are we willing to take the risk?

Psalm 8

Psalm 8 is all about risk. It is about the risk God takes in sharing with human beings the care for the created order. Psalm 8 is usually classified as a hymn to God the Creator, because it expresses the theme of orientation, of a secure, well-ordered, trustworthy, no-surprise world. I would like to treat it here as a psalm of new orientation, of surprise, of new life on the other side of the pit experience. I want to focus upon Psalm 8 as a tool, not of social control and the status quo, but of social critique and transformation. There is an eschatological picture in Psalm 8, which calls us back to God's intentions for us and empowers our lives as human beings. It speaks of our becoming rather than of our being. If Psalm 8 is proclaimed, heard, and believed as a psalm of divine risk, it challenges us to reconsider our way in the world and with each other.

Psalm 8 gives powerful testimony about creation (cosmology), God (theology), and human beings (anthropology). It can be broken down into the three-part hymn structure that we studied in chapter 2: introduction, body, and conclusion (or the summons to praise, the motive or reason for praise, and the renewed call to praise). The introduction in verse 1a is not a call to praise but rather a declaration about God that would naturally evoke praise: "O Adonai, our ruler, how majestic is your name in all the earth!" This declaration is repeated in the final verse, 9, creating a powerful envelope structure. What is inserted in the envelope in verses 1b–8 explains concretely what it means to claim that God's name is majestic.

Majesty has to do with God's all-encompassing power and presence. This is seen in the use of "all" as the main, thematic, key word of the psalm: "all the earth" in verses 1 and 9 and "all under [humankind's] feet" in verse 6. "Heavens" in verse 1b links with "earth" in verse 1a to reinforce the idea of "allness," of inclusiveness, and recalls the creation story in Genesis 1, where "heaven and earth" is the biblical idiom for "all of creation."[13]

Verse 1b begins the body of the hymn, which gives the reason for the declaration and praise and which continues through verse 8. Verses 1b and 2 are difficult to translate from the Hebrew because of the words' uncertain meanings. The introduction may continue beyond verse 1a, depending upon how an English translator punctuates the verses, with a period or with no period after 1b (the Hebrew text itself does not contain any periods or semicolons). The options for verses 1b and 2 include: "Thou whose glory above the heavens is chanted by the mouth of babes and infants, thou hast founded a bulwark because of thy foes, to still the enemy and the avenger [RSV]" or "You whose glory above the heavens is chanted. By the mouth of babes and infants at the breast you have founded a bulwark against your foes, to still the enemy and the avenger."

With the second translation, the poet feels God's power working even in the praise of little children; and God's enemies, those who deny God's power and refuse to recognize the majesty of God's name, are overcome by that power. That is, God's name is majestic precisely because it is revealed in small things. Children's praise has great power. Jesus recognized this in the cries of the little children who shouted "Hosanna to the son of David" upon his entry into Jerusalem: "Out of the mouths of babes and sucklings you have brought perfect praise [Matt. 21:16, RSV]" (compare with Paul's remarks in 2 Corinthians 12:9). Verse 2 of the psalm pulls us in from the idea of God's name, majestic throughout the whole earth, to the human being. There is dignity and challenge for the human being in this contrast.

In verses 3 and 4, the psalmist seems overwhelmed by the grandeur of creation and the Creator: "When I look at your heavens, the work of your fingers, the moon and the stars which you have set in place, what is [the human being] that you are mindful of [her], and the mortal person that you care for [him]?" Human beings seem inconsequential in comparison to the expanse of the heavens and God's creation. What a difference between God the Creator and the creature is revealed by a look at the stars!

Note that verse 3 shows a movement of specification: The psalmist looks at the heavens (3a) and then at what is contained within the heavens, the moon and the stars (3b). There is also vertical movement between verses 3 and 4; the psalmist's gaze moves down from the heavens to the earth, to human beings. The Hebrew for *man* (RSV) in verse 4a, *enosh*, is found mostly in poetic texts and can mean humans, humankind, or a single person. It comes from a verb root that means to be weak or sick. The Hebrew in verse 4b for *son of man* (RSV), *ben-adam* (literally, "child of a human being") occurs frequently in Ezekiel to underscore the difference between the human, mortal, earthly being and the infinite, immortal, and powerful God. Thus we have a movement of intensification in the nouns of verse 4a and 4b.

This stress on the smallness and insignificance of human beings is somewhat countered by the verbs of verse 4, "remember" or "be mindful of" and "care for" or "visit," which also show a movement of intensification. This intensification juxtaposes the majesty of the creator God with the intimate care of the deliverer God. This intimate relationship between Creator and creature is underscored by the use of "work of your fingers" in verse 3a, a variation of the usual "work of your hands" found for God's creation in the psalms. "Fingers" suggests more delicate work, more care and tenderness. God is not only over all as Creator, majestically enthroned in the heavens, but is also intimately connected with God's creation, tending it, caring for it. This is a source of awe and wonder for the psalmist of Psalm 8 as it is for the psalmist of 144 (verse 3).

It is striking that the verbs "be mindful of" and "care for" in Psalm 8:4 are also found frequently in lament psalms, especially in the petitions. The psalmist pleads with God to "be mindful of me and care for me" (as in Jeremiah's lament in Jeremiah 15:15). The laments plead for this intimacy, which is not being experienced in the pit of disorientation. Also, Job 7:17–19 offers a bitter parody of the verbs in Psalm 8: "What is the [human being] that you make so much of him, and that you set your mind on [her], visit him every morning and test [her] every moment? How long will you not look away from me, nor let me be until I swallow my spittle?" Job would prefer it if God left him alone and didn't pay so much attention to him. For Job, God no longer seems concerned in an intimate and positive way toward God's creation. Job is not experiencing God's order and tenderness and care. God's concern has become a torment to Job, as it is for the psalmist in Psalm 39:13.

Despite the inconsequence of human beings in the vast expanse of the created order, the psalmist of Psalm 8 admits that God has given human beings an extraordinary place in creation: "Yet you have made [us] little less than God and crown [us] with glory and splendor [5]." This is royal language, the language of enthrone-ment, but it is used for human beings, not for God or the earthly sovereign. The sense of human insignificance expressed in verse 3 is challenged by the puzzled question of verse 4 (about how God could care for such an insignificant one) and then decisively overturned by the assertion of verse 5. The "yet" of verse 5 underscores this juxtaposition of frail creature with gifted one "little less than God."

It is alarming to note how many English translators back away from the bold claim of verse 5 that God has made us "little less than God [rsv]." Some translate it "little less than gods" or "little less than a god," meaning, perhaps, the deities who don't really count in the ancient Near East. Other translations, such as Jerome's Vulgate, use "little less than angels" (the reading in the note of JPS offers "divine" instead of "angels" in the main text). This reading seems to claim a little less for humankind. All of these translations are possible except "angels," for which another Hebrew word is usually used. The Hebrew in Psalm 8 is *elohim*, one of the names for God but also the word for the gods of Canaan. We seem to be quite uncomfortable with the challenge of being "little less than God," yet this is what is also implied by Genesis 1, which asserts that we have been made in God's image and given dominion over creation. Perhaps in its assessment of human nature as corrupt and sinful, Christian anthropology with its "worm theology," a legacy of Augustine and the early church, leaves no room for this empowering view of humankind.

Verse 6 specifies the meaning of the crowning of the human creature made little less than God: "You have given [us] dominion over the works of your hands; you have put all things under [our] feet." In verses 7 and 8, that dominion is detailed: "sheep, oxen, beasts of the field, birds of the air, fish of the sea." Creatures in the three spheres of the created order are named to specify what "all things under our feet" means. Again, the sense of "all," of the whole created order, is communicated.

The discussion of the place of human beings in God's creation and of the dominion given human beings over the earth immediately calls to mind the Genesis 1 creation story. In Genesis 1:26, after God creates an orderly world out of chaos, male and female are created in God's image and given dominion over the earth. In both Genesis 1 and Psalm 8, the human being is seen as made for relationship with God, which involves human dominion over the created order. Some theologians have argued that Psalm 8 is a commentary on Genesis 1, but Brueggemann argues that the influence could be in the other direction: "The narrative derives from the doxology."[14] In one look up at the heavens, the psalmist brings into play all at once questions, awe, and sense of self. The poetry of Psalm 8 offers us a simultaneous and synthetic view of God, the world, and our place in the world, rather than a sequential or a narrative description.

This view of the dignity of human beings in Psalm 8 was nothing short of revolutionary in the ancient Near East among Israel's neighbors. The gods of these other nations personified the powers of nature like wind, lightning, rain, the sea. All significant activity was located in the heavenly realm of the gods. The gods had dominion over the earth; humans served the gods and had to pattern their earthly life after the heavenly. Humans were servants of the gods in the ancient Near Eastern myths, doing the dirty work the gods felt themselves too good to do.

In Genesis 1 and Psalm 8, however, human beings assume the role of the gods. This is the source of awe and wonder in the psalm. Human significance is the gift of the creator God, Adonai, who cares for us. God gives humankind dominion over the earth. This is what makes us little less than God. The fact that God takes a risk in giving us dominion over the earth can be seen in the debate over what *dominion* means in Psalm 8 and Genesis 1. Phyllis Trible[15] argues that some people insist that dominion is a license to plunder, abuse, and pollute the earth and ravage one another as we please: they blame the present ecological crisis on Genesis 1.

A close reading of Genesis 1, however, shows that dominion is God's good gift. We are trustees and stewards of God's creation, responsible for the ongoing health of God's world. Our separation from nature does not mean that we must be antagonistic toward it. Separation is part of the fabric of creation, night separated from day by the lights, the waters separated by the firmament, plants and animals differentiated according to their kind. Dominion is not alienation but harmonious control. Dominion is a limited gift. It is checked and defined by the context of the affirmation of the goodness and harmony of creation. Over all is God, who establishes order and delegates responsibilities.

The very structure of Psalm 8 makes this point. The psalmist does not dwell on human significance. The envelope of praise of God's majestic name in verses 1 and 9 makes our human centeredness, our self-centeredness impossible. Lest we focus only on ourselves, in verses 5–8, the psalmist pulls us out of ourselves and back to God and in verse 9 repeats the opening declaration about God's majestic name. Human dignity points to God who has granted that dignity. Psalm 8 focuses on God, the Creator; creation and human beings are secondary, pointing back to God. This God-focus puts human beings and the created order in right relationship to God and one another. As Brueggemann puts it, "Doxology gives dominion its context and legitimacy."[16] Psalm 8 centers us on God and calls us to a dominion of responsible stewardship and trusteeship. Our modern, self-centered, technological society, which operates under the illusion that we are in control, would do well to heed the warning and challenge of Psalm 8.

How can the human creature responsibly exercise dominion over all of God's magnificent creation? Harrelson[17] suggests that we can do so by "being made whole, made new, opened up to the powers of divine creativity" in our acts of celebration and worship. In worship, "the beauty and the terror" of God's presence and of our "mixed-up world" are laid bare. Worship confronts us with the consequences of our disobedience and with the risk God has taken in giving us responsibility in our exercise of dominion. Worship does not allow us to leave the world outside at the front door of the church. In worship we examine ourselves and our lives in God's presence. Mysteriously, we are renewed for our God-given task.

If liturgy constructs worlds, as Brueggemann maintains, then Psalm 8 can generate a new world, the world that God intends for us, in the very moment of its use in worship. The new world is an eschatological world of responsible stewardship and God-centeredness. It lures us. As Harrelson states: "Capacity to receive the world as God's world, capacity to exult in its good and to grieve over its wounds, capacity to take our place in its order-being-established—this is what we most profoundly want."[18] This is what awaits us in worship if we but risk it, if we want it enough. This is what makes us whole. A journey through the psalms—hymns, wisdom psalms, laments, thanksgivings, enthronement psalms—is a path to wholeness, a way of constructing this new world in our liturgies. Within this new world that God intends, we are free to become, to be all that God intends us to be; we are whole and healthy persons.

God, the Holy One, has invited us to join in this process of world building through our worship, which empowers us. The psalms used in our worship can express the full range of our humanness, our pain, our anger, our joy, our hopes, our thanks. Psalms engage us as whole persons and thus can help us to deal honestly with God, one another, and our world, making us better world builders. How we hear and use the psalms affects greatly the kind of world we build. The psalms present us with eschatological pictures, if we would but open ourselves to them, of a world even now coming into being. How full of wonder that is! Hallelujah!

Notes

Chapter 1—Who Needs the Psalms Anyway?

1. A. Duba, "Psalms, the Scripture and the Church," *Liturgy* 3, 3 (1983): 35.
2. *Jesus Christ—The Life of the World*, a worship book for the Sixth Assembly of the World Council of Churches (Geneva, 1983).
3. Harold Kushner, *Who Needs God?* (New York: Summit Books, 1989), 9. Kushner argues that it is the psalms that provide the kind of nourishment that our souls crave. From praying the psalms we get a sense of being in God's presence that reassures us that we are not alone, and also, we come to terms with our human limitations.
4. David Willis, "Contemporary Theology and Prayer," *Interpretation* 34 (1980): 250–64. Willis argues for the strong correlation between a theologian's doctrine of prayer and his or her doctrine of God.
5. Don Saliers, "Prayer and the Doctrine of God in Contemporary Theology," *Interpretation* 34 (1980): 278. This criterion of "prayability" is clearly absent in Kushner's best-seller *When Bad Things Happen to Good People* (New York: Schocken Books, 1981). In his picture of God, Kushner leaves little room for the psalm lament and thus for the full range of prayer.
6. Roland Murphy, "The Faith of the Psalmist," *Interpretation* 34 (1980): 237.
7. Ibid., 236.
8. Walter Brueggemann, "From Hurt to Joy, from Death to Life," *Interpretation* 28 (1974): 4.
9. Gordon Lathrop, "A Rebirth of Images: On the Use of the Bible in Liturgy," *Worship* 58 (1984): 299.
10. Even the liturgical Psalter (for which I served as a reader/reviewer

127

before its final editing) in the new *United Methodist Hymnal* (Nashville: The United Methodist Publishing House, 1989), is guilty of this practice. Despite the fact that laments like Pss. 13 and 137 stand, thankfully, in their entirety, others like 44 and 77 do not. In the case of Ps. 44, only vv. 1–8 are included, which declare God's saving acts in the past; this testimony serves to heighten the anguish of the following excluded verses, which describe God's very different present conduct. The contrast functions as the basis for the psalmist's appeal.

11. See, for example, Donald Gowan, *Reclaiming the Old Testament for the Christian Pulpit* (Atlanta: John Knox Press, 1976). Gowan treats the psalms in the epilogue, arguing that form criticism can help one preach from different parts of Hebrew Scripture but not from the psalms.

12. Erhard Gerstenberger, "Enemies and Evildoers in the Psalms: A Challenge to Christian Preaching," *Horizons in Biblical Theology* 4–5 (1982–83): 77. Even Claus Westermann, who argues that we must take psalms as they are, maintains that some psalms contain features that "we cannot directly adopt as our own prayer, in particular the petitions against enemies" in individual laments (*The Living Psalms* [Grand Rapids: Eerdmans, 1989], 2).

13. Patrick Miller, *Interpreting the Psalms* (Philadelphia: Fortress Press, 1986), 21.

14. Roy Harrisville, "Paul and the Psalms: A Formal Study," *Word and World*, 5, 2 (1985): 168–80.

15. The Hebrew word *ḥesed* is usually translated as "steadfast love" or "mercy," but is better translated as "covenant love" or "loyalty." I use the terms B.C.E., Before the Common Era, and C.E., the Common Era, in place of the confessional terms, B.C., Before Christ, and A.D., Anno Domino (year of our Lord), in order to encourage dialogue between Christians and people of other faiths, especially Jews, who do not confess Jesus as Lord. My use of the term *Hebrew Scripture* for what Christians call the Old Testament reflects this same concern. The use of *Old Testament* can make it easy for Christians to forget that Jews address different questions to scripture and allow the witness of the first part of the Christian Bible to inform their lives in different ways than Christians. The term *Hebrew Scripture* acknowledges that these are writings, originally in Hebrew, that are normative, or canonical, for more than one faith community, i.e., for both Jews and Christians. See Denise D. Hopkins, "God's Continuing Covenant with the Jews and the Christian Reading of the Bible," *Prism* 3, 2 (1988), 60–75.

16. Shaye Cohen, *From the Maccabees to the Mishnah* (Philadelphia: Westminster Press, 1987).

17. R. Posner, U. Kaploun, and S. Cohen, eds., *Jewish Liturgy, Prayer and Synagogue Service Through the Ages* (Jerusalem: Keter Publishing House, 1975), 18–19. Statutory prayer is recited to fulfill an obligation to pray rather than to mark a special occasion or event. *Midrash* is a term for rabbinic biblical interpretation. *Talmud* (study) is rabbinic commentary on the Mishnah (a collection of legal statements from the rabbis of the second century C.E.), produced in both Palestine and Babylonia between the third and sixth centuries C.E.

18. Geoffrey Wainwright, *Doxology: The Praise of God in Worship, Doctrine and Life* (New York: Oxford University Press, 1980), 210.

19. Quoted in Massey H. Shepherd, *The Psalms in Christian Worship, A Practical Guide* (Minneapolis: Augsburg, 1976), 37.

20. Shepherd, 39.

21. Cohen, *From the Maccabees*, 68–69. A third prayer, which did not parallel the sacrificial cult, was recommended but not required. It is uncertain to what extent the rabbinic injunctions reflected the actual situation in the Second Temple period. The *Tamid* was God's "daily food," an honoring of God's presence in the Temple.

22. Shepherd, *The Psalms*, 54–55. In a manual of church order (c. 200 C.E.), Hippolytus of Rome outlined the six prayer times: (1) dawn—pray upon rising; (2) third hour (9 a.m.)—recall that Christ was nailed to the cross; (3) sixth hour (noon)—darkness covered the earth; (4) ninth hour (3 P.M.)—the Lord was pierced and died; (5) evening—pray before sleep; (6) midnight—arise and pray, for at this hour the Bridegroom comes. Shepherd notes that we do not know how many Christians followed this discipline or what exactly they prayed when they did; possibly the psalms were recited, along with the Lord's Prayer and Bible passages.

23. Donald Hustad, "The Psalms as Worship Expression: Personal and Congregational," *Review and Expositor* 81, 3 (1984): 414.

24. The NEB, New English Bible, does not include the Book I, Book II, etc. designations. This was a modern editorial decision. The five-fold psalm division mirrors the five-fold division of the Torah (or Pentateuch, the first five books of Hebrew Scripture), which was made in the Second Temple period.

25. In the same way, the new *United Methodist Hymnal* brings together Methodist and Evangelical United Brethren hymns and traditions, which had been circulating independently.

26. Miller, *Interpreting the Psalms*, 45.

27. G. Wilson, *The Editing of the Hebrew Psalter* (Chico, Calif.: Scholars Press, 1985), argues that psalm superscriptions about David were added to psalms with cultic, technical superscription terminology in order to obscure their original cultic matrix and ensure individual access to the psalms. This "move toward personalization" argument

unfairly denies the possibility that there can be pious and personal moments in Israelite worship.

28. Sigmund Mowinckel, *The Psalms in Israel's Worship*, 2 vols. (Nashville: Abingdon Press, 1962). Artur Weiser, *The Psalms*, Old Testament Library (Philadelphia: Westminster Press, 1962).

29. Claus Westermann, *Praise and Lament in the Psalms* (Atlanta: John Knox Press, 1981), 122.

30. Brueggemann, *The Message of the Psalms* (Minneapolis: Augsburg, 1984), 19.

Chapter 2—Your Hallelujahs Don't Have to Be Hollow Anymore

1. Geoffrey Wainwright, *Doxology: The Praise of God in Worship, Doctrine and Life* (New York: Oxford University Press, 1980), 8.

2. Walter Brueggemann, *The Message of the Psalms* (Minneapolis: Augsburg, 1984), 19.

3. Ronald Clements, *In Spirit and in Truth* (Atlanta: John Knox Press, 1985), 13–14.

4. Patrick Miller, *Interpreting the Psalms* (Philadelphia: Fortress Press, 1986), 64.

5. Bruce Birch, *Singing the Lord's Song: A Study of Isaiah 40—55* (Nashville: Abingdon Press, 1989), 83.

6. Brueggemann, *The Message of the Psalms*, 55. This motivation assumes a kind of parity in the relationship between God and the psalmist.

7. Birch, *Singing the Lord's Song*, 83–85.

8. Claus Westermann, *Praise and Lament in the Psalms* (Atlanta: John Knox Press, 1981), 116–42.

9. Miller, *Interpreting the Psalms*, 66.

10. Ibid., 67.

11. Brueggemann, "From Hurt to Joy, from Death to Life," *Interpretation* 28 (1974): 13–18.

12. Miller, *Interpreting the Psalms*, 68.

13. Brueggemann, *The Message of the Psalms*, 26.

14. Ibid., 27.

15. Wainwright, *Doxology*, 425.

16. Ibid., 118–21.

17. Brueggemann, *The Message of the Psalms*, 28.

18. James H. Cone, "Sanctification, Liberation and Black Worship," *Theology Today*, 35 (1978–79), 140.

19. Brueggemann, *Israel's Praise: Doxology Against Idolatry and Ideology* (Philadelphia: Fortress Press, 1989).

20. Miller, *Interpreting the Psalms*, 70.

21. Brueggemann, *The Message of the Psalms*, 30.

22. Miller, *Interpreting the Psalms*, 71.
23. Katharine Sakenfeld, *Faithfulness in Action: Loyalty in Biblical Perspective* (Philadelphia: Fortress Press, 1985).
24. Miller, *Interpreting the Psalms*, 73.
25. Ibid., 75.
26. Brueggemann, *The Message of the Psalms*, 36.
27. Bernhard Anderson, *Out of the Depths: The Psalms Speak for Us Today*, rev. and enl. (Philadelphia: Westminster Press, 1983), 53.
28. Ibid., 148.
29. Artur Weiser, *The Psalms* (Philadelphia: Westminster Press, 1962), 481.
30. Weiser, *The Psalms*, 55. Gerhard von Rad, in his *Old Testament Theology* vol. 2 (Edinburgh: Oliver and Boyd, 1965), characterizes the whole Psalter as Israel's "response" to God.
31. James Pritchard, *Ancient Near Eastern Texts Relating to the Old Testament*, 3d ed. (Princeton: Princeton University Press, 1969), 369–73.
32. Anderson, *Out of the Depths*, 158.
33. Leslie A. Allen, *Psalms 101–150*, Word Biblical Commentary, vol. 21 (Waco, Tex.: Word Books, 1983), 32–33.
34. Harvey Guthrie, *Israel's Sacred Songs* (New York: Seabury Press, 1978), 61ff., for what follows. Guthrie's book has been reprinted by University Press of America.
35. Note the sound correspondence between *tehom* and Tiamat, the goddess of the salt sea (representing the power of chaos) in the Babylonian creation myth. Tiamat is vanquished by the young storm God Marduk, who becomes the head of the divine assembly of the gods. The battle between them results in the creation of the world out of Tiamat's body.
36. Leslie C. Allen, *Psalms 101–150*, 34.
37. Brueggemann, *The Message of the Psalms*, 32.
38. Allen, *Psalms 101–150*, 33.
39. Brueggemann, *The Message of the Psalms*, 33.
40. Guthrie, *Israel's Sacred Songs*, 66–69.
41. Joseph Campbell, *The Power of Myth*, with Bill Moyers (New York: Doubleday, 1988), 40. Unfortunately, Campbell argues (page 31) that the myth of the West does not function today, because it is based on the Bible and its view of the universe that belongs to the first millenium B.C.E.; "it does not accord with our concept either of the universe or of the dignity of man [sic]." I would argue rather that our Western myth is in trouble precisely because it is not based upon the Bible, but rather upon an Enlightenment view of inevitable progress. The Bible appropriately interpreted can help us to recover what Campbell sees as the "mystical function" of myth, "realizing what a

wonder the universe is, and what a wonder you are, and experiencing awe before this mystery" (31). The psalms lift up the dignity of the human being and our awe before the Creator. See my treatment of Psalm 8 in chapter 6.

42. Robert Alter, *The Art of Biblical Poetry* (New York: Basic Books, 1985), 121.

43. Peter Craigie, *Psalms 1–50*, Word Biblical Commentary, vol. 19 (Waco, Tex.: Word Books, 1983), 343.

44. Walter Harrelson, *From Fertility Cult to Worship* (Missoula, Mont.: Scholars Press, reprint of 1969 Doubleday ed), 137–47.

45. Ibid., 138.

46. Ibid., 150.

47. My thanks to Dee Ann Dixon, a student at Wesley Theological Seminary, for this thoughtful insight.

Chapter 3—You Get What You Deserve, Don't You?

1. Walter Brueggemann, *The Message of the Psalms* (Minneapolis: Augsburg, 1984), 38.

2. Peter Craigie, *Psalms 1–50*, Word Biblical Commentary, vol. 19 (Waco, Tex.: Word Books, 1983), 180. For the interpretation that follows, see 182–83.

3. For what follows, see John Collins, *Proverbs/Ecclesiastes*, Knox Preaching Guides (Atlanta: John Knox Press, 1980), 1–14.

4. Cf. Proverbs 10:3; 12:7; 13:9; 13:21; 14:11; 15:16; 15:29; 24:16; 26:27.

5. Brueggemann, *The Message of the Psalms*, 38–39; n. 32, 183.

6. Fred B. Craddock, "Hearing God's Blessing," *The Christian Century* (January 1990): 74.

7. Ibid.

8. Craigie, *Psalms 1–50*, 61.

9. Robert Alter, *The Art of Biblical Poetry* (New York: Basic Books, 1985), 115–17.

10. Brueggemann, *The Message of the Psalms*, 42.

Chapter 4—Complaining in Faith to God

1. Roland Murphy, "The Faith of the Psalmist," *Interpretation* 34 (1980): 236.

2. Walter Brueggemann, *The Message of the Psalms* (Minneapolis: Augsburg, 1984), 22.

3. Craig Broyles, *The Conflict of Faith and Experience in the Psalms*, JSOT

Supplement Series 52 (Sheffield, England: Sheffield Academic Press, 1989), 14.

4. Harold Kushner, *When Bad Things Happen to Good People* (New York: Schocken Books, 1981), 88.

5. Broyles, *Faith and Experience*, 81.

6. Wayne Oates, *The Presence of God in Pastoral Counseling* (Waco, Tex.: Word Books, 1986), 105–106.

7. Brueggemann, *The Message of the Psalms*, 55.

8. Murphy, "The Faith of the Psalmist," 238.

9. Erhard Gerstenberger, "Enemies and Evildoers in the Psalms: A Challenge to Christian Preaching," *Horizons in Biblical Theology* 4–5 (1982–83): 61–77.

10. David Briggs, Associated Press, "Debate over Abortion Rights Revives Hell as Topic of Religious Discussion," *The Washington Post*, 24 February 1990.

11. Dorothee Soelle, *Suffering*, trans. E. Kalin (Philadelphia: Fortress Press, 1975), 4.

12. Brueggemann, *The Message of the Psalms*, 168–69.

13. Ibid., 171.

14. Ibid., 175.

15. Ibid., 77.

16. Dietrich Bonhoeffer, *The Cost of Discipleship*, trans. R.H. Fuller (New York: Macmillan, 1963), 45, 54.

17. Brueggemann, *The Message of the Psalms*, 176.

18. Broyles, *Faith and Experience*, 70–73.

19. Ibid., 66.

20. Pierre Wolff, *May I Hate God?* (New York: Paulist Press, 1979): 25.

21. Daniel Simundson, *Faith Under Fire: Biblical Interpretations of Suffering* (Minneapolis: Augsburg, 1980), 48.

22. Robert Mcaffee Brown, *Creation Dislocation: The Movement of Grace* (Nashville, Abingdon Press, 1980), 89.

23. Elie Wiesel, *Night* (New York: Bantam Books, 1982), 61.

24. Kushner, *When Bad Things Happen*, 108.

25. Ibid., 37.

26. William Sloan Coffin, Jr., "My Son Beat Me to the Grave," *AD Magazine* (June 1983): 25–26.

27. Richard F. Vieth, *Holy Power, Human Pain* (Bloomington, Ind.: Meyer-Stone Books, 1988), 17–25.

28. Broyles, *Faith and Experience*, 113.

29. Ibid., 131.

30. Brueggemann, *The Message of the Psalms*, 104.

31. Claus Westermann, "The Role of the Lament in the Theology of the Old Testament," *Interpretation* 28, 1 (1974): 33.

32. Simundson, *Faith Under Fire*, 50.
33. Brueggemann, *The Message of the Psalms*, 55.
34. Ibid., 55.
35. Ibid., 55.

Chapter 5—Life in the Meanwhile

1. Walter Brueggemann, *The Message of the Psalms* (Minneapolis: Augsburg, 1984), 56.
2. Brueggemann, "From Hurt to Joy, from Death to Life," *Interpretation* 28, 1 (1974): 10, 13.
3. Ibid., 18.
4. Claus Westermann, "The Role of the Lament in the Theology of the Old Testament," *Interpretation* 28, 1 (1974): 27.
5. Pierre Wolff, *May I Hate God?* (New York: Paulist Press, 1979): 57.
6. Ibid., 34.
7. Ibid., 57.
8. My thanks to Marcia Cox, a Doctor of Ministry candidate at Wesley Seminary, for this insight from Melville.
9. Nelle Morton, *The Journey Is Home* (Boston: Beacon Press, 1985), 127–28.
10. Ibid., 129.
11. Dorothee Soelle, *Suffering* (Philadelphia: Fortress Press, 1975), 70, 76.
12. Daniel Simundson, *Faith Under Fire* (Minneapolis: Augsburg, 1980), 61.
13. Elizabeth Kuebler-Ross, *On Death and Dying* (New York: Macmillan, 1969). A physician describes five stages of coping for those terminally ill: denial and isolation, anger, bargaining, depression, and acceptance. Those grieving the loss of a loved one "undergo different stages of adjustment similar to the ones described for our patients" (149).
14. Cited in "Facing Life Alone Again," by Rhoda Donkin, *Washington Post Health*, 10 January 1989, 16.
15. Ibid.
16. Ken Denlinger, "Gibbs: 'Emotional Marathon'," *The Washington Post*, 12 November 1989, B1.
17. Simundson, *Faith Under Fire*, 97.
18. Ibid., 98.
19. Brueggemann, *The Message of the Psalms*, 56.
20. William Sloan Coffin, Jr. "My Son Beat Me to the Grave," *AD Magazine* (June 1983): 26.
21. Samuel E. Balentine, *The Hidden God: The Hiding of the Face of God in the Old Testament* (Oxford: Oxford University Press, 1983), 166.
22. Ibid.

23. Ibid., 173.
24. Robert Alter, *The Art of Biblical Poetry* (New York: Basic Books, 1985), 63.
25. Craig Broyles, *The Conflict of Faith and Experience in the Psalms*, JSOT Supplement Series 52 (Sheffield, England: Sheffield Academic Press, 1989), 31–34.
26. Brueggemann, *The Message of the Psalms*, 68.

Chapter 6—I'll Never Be the Same Again

1. Walter Brueggemann, *The Message of the Psalms* (Minneapolis: Augsburg, 1984), 175.
2. Ibid., 124.
3. Brueggemann, *Israel's Praise: Doxology Against Idolatry and Ideology* (Philadelphia: Fortress Press, 1988), 148.
4. Ibid.
5. Ibid., 29.
6. Artur Weiser, *The Psalms*. Old Testament Library (Philadelphia: Westminster Press, 1962), 376.
7. Peter Craigie, *Psalms 1–50*, Word Biblical Commentary, vol. 19 (Waco, Tex.: Word Books, 1983), 349.
8. Brueggemann, *Israel's Praise*, 34.
9. Ibid., 36.
10. Ibid., 38.
11. Ibid., 55.
12. Ibid., 63, 68.
13. Robert Alter, *The Art of Biblical Poetry* (New York: Basic Books, 1985), 119.
14. Brueggemann, *The Message of the Psalms*, n. 29, 183.
15. Phyllis Trible, "Ancient Priests and Modern Polluters," *Andover-Newton Quarterly* 12 (1971).
16. Brueggemann, *The Message of the Psalms*, 38.
17. Walter Harrelson, *From Fertility Cult to Worship* (Missoula, Mont.: Scholars Press, reprint of 1969 Doubleday ed), 96–97.
18. Ibid., 99.

Bibliography

Allen, Leslie. *Psalms 101–150.* Word Biblical Commentary, vol. 21. Waco, Tex.: Word Books, 1983.

Anderson, Bernhard. *Out of the Depths: The Psalms Speak for Us Today.* Rev. Philadelphia: Westminster Press, 1983.

Brueggemann, Walter. *The Message of the Psalms: A Theological Commentary.* Minneapolis: Augsburg, 1984.

Craigie, Peter. *Psalms 1–50.* Word Biblical Commentary, vol. 19. Waco, Tex.: Word Books, 1983.

Griggs, Donald. *Praying and Teaching the Psalms.* Nashville: Abingdon Press, 1984.

Guthrie, Harvey. *Israel's Sacred Songs: A Study of Dominant Themes.* New York: Seabury Press, 1966.

Miller, Patrick. *Interpreting the Psalms.* Philadelphia: Fortress Press, 1986.

Weiser, Artur. *The Psalms.* Philadelphia: Westminster Press, 1962.

Westermann, Claus. *Praise and Lament in the Psalms.* Atlanta: John Knox Press, 1981.

The Writings (Ketubim), A New Translation of The Holy Scriptures. Philadelphia: The Jewish Publication Society of America, 1982.